10

SECRETS
TO SPORTING
SUCCESS

Professionals reveal their
mind training secrets.
Follow this step-by-step
guide to reach your true
potential and to coach
others to reach theirs.

KATIE PAGE & HELEN CLARKE

10 Secrets to Sporting Success

First published in 2015 by

Panoma Press Ltd

48 St Vincent Drive, St Albans, Herts, AL1 5SJ, UK
info@panomapress.com
www.panomapress.com

Book layout by Neil Coe

Printed on acid-free paper from managed forests.

ISBN 978-1-909623-79-8

The right of Katie Page & Helen Clarke to be identified as the authors of this work has been asserted in accordance with sections 77 and 78 of the Copyright Designs and Patents Act 1988.

A CIP catalogue record for this book is available from the British Library.

This book is available online and in bookstores.

For our families, friends and participants in sports everywhere with a special dedication for Tom, Charlie, Graham, Ross and James who support us in everything we do.

CONTENTS

INTRODUCTION

Welcome to '10 Secrets to Sporting Success'.

Let us explain the formula of this book and how to get the most from it.

Working with athletes and sportspeople of all levels and abilities, we realised there were a number of areas and tools that made a huge difference to their performance and training. These ten areas became our ten chapters.

Each chapter begins with an interview with a sports professional. These professionals describe how important that particular aspect of mind training is to them and give you a tip that has helped them achieve the great success that they have had.

We are very grateful for their enthusiastic support of our project.

The chapters also contain a secret backed up by science and facts. There are a number of mind training tools for you to learn and use throughout the book. If you are serious about making the most of this book and the secrets held within it you will need to get fully involved. The more you put into this, the more you will get out of it and the greater the difference you will make to your performance.

"Wherever the mind goes, the body will follow"

This is one of the foundations of mind training. As you move through this book it will become a lot more apparent how connected your mind and your body are. Also, you will learn how to take greater control of both your mind and your body. By doing this you will naturally achieve greater results and more consistency in your performance.

So often the mind is neglected and all the focus is upon the physical. If you work on them both together, you will be able to unlock your peak potential.

Mind training is like physical training – you can work on it and you can always improve.

You would not go into a competition without any physical training or some sort of warm up, would you? If this is the case, why would you do that with your mind? If you have the right tools you can train your mind and body to be in their peak performance state. This will allow them to perform together to their best ability.

Ask yourself how much you think your mind impacts your performance when you compete, as a percentage. Is it over 50%? Research shows it is actually 75% or higher. Think of the difference training your mind could make to your performance.

The key to mind training is to keep things simple. So often we can bombard our brains with too many thoughts. At the end of the day, this is about you having a better understanding of you as a person and equipping yourself with the right tools to help you reach your true potential.

Your Mind Training Log Book:

When going through this book, it is really important to write things down. Please use a small notepad which will ideally fit into your kit bag.

Research by the Dominican University of California shows us that those people who write down their goals in detail achieve significantly more than those who don't. This notebook will become your mind training journal which we will show you how to use alongside your training, leading up to and also during and after a competition.

As you go through these chapters, we will provide you with certain exercises to write down, but we also highly recommend that you take notes of anything that you think is particularly relevant to you; certain quotes that inspire you or particular learnings that you feel will really help you.

Many successful athletes have invested the time and energy they need into training their minds alongside their bodies. Congratulations, buying this book and working through it shows that you too have recognised its importance and the benefit you can gain from it.

We really hope you enjoy the journey.

CHAPTER ONE:

THOUGHT PROCESSES

Alison Rose, physiotherapist to Jessica Ennis-Hill and
Dame Kelly Holmes.

Alison has worked at four Olympic Games with a variety
of athletes including Jessica Ennis-Hill at London 2012.
Ali has been working as a physiotherapist in sports for the
last nineteen years. She has worked with UK Athletics as
a consultant since 2000, working at the Olympics with
athletics in 2000, 2004 and 2008, and 2012. She has also
worked at the World Championships in athletics in 2001,
2003, 2005, 2007 and 2009, the European Championships
in athletics in 2002 and 2006, as well as the World and
European Cross Country Championships since 2003. Ali
is the physiotherapist credited with helping to keep Dame
Kelly Holmes injury free in the two years leading up to the
Athens Olympics in 2004, enabling her to achieve double
Olympic gold in the 800m and 1500m.

Alison's View on Thought Processes:

I feel that beyond physical talent, the power of the mind is the single biggest thing that could affect performance and is hugely underrated. It should be worked on as much as any other type of training. Through my work with athletes and non-athletes, I have seen incredibly talented people not reaching their potential in competition through lack of confidence in their fitness, themselves, their bodies, or their belief that they don't deserve to beat the person standing next to them on the start line. The mind can be closed to the possibility that you can win, or that you can achieve above and beyond what your training suggests on paper, or that you should dare to beat the next person.

I have seen top athletes who have had many injuries live in fear of being injured again and not performing because of this, and I have noticed changes in their physical performance as their confidence grows when they no longer have long-term or recurrent injuries. I have seen athletes who live in the physio room the week before a big race with an injury that miraculously disappears on race day, and feel that this may be an unconscious excuse, should they not perform.

I have also seen athletes who are unable to focus on their own performance in competition, who aren't present in the moment, fail to perform and get the best out of themselves. This can be because they are too focussed on another competitor who they assume will probably beat them, or they miss out on qualification because they are too focussed on what they may do in the final.

Conversely, I have also had the pleasure of working with athletes of all standards who have been able to make the right decisions, believe in themselves and dare to raise their game beyond their wildest dreams, seizing the moment and performing to the highest level that they can.

Alison's Tip for Sporting Success:

You can only affect the outcome of your own performance. No amount of worrying about anyone else will affect their performance and will only adversely affect your own. At my first senior cross country international, I was very nervous about my own ability, and how I might perform having never competed at this level before. I was really worried about another athlete who talked about her great times in training and how fit she was. Luckily I saw her warming up and realised that she was probably not being totally honest. It gave me the confidence to put her right out of my mind. Consequently, I was the first girl back in our team. The girl I had worried about was last. I knew from then on, as long as I had done all of the training set by my coach, was healthy and I did my absolute best and focused on that, I could do no more.

One thing I have learnt from others is that the better the athlete you are, the more you need to address all aspects of performance in order to get the best out of yourself. Psychology is a vital part of this. It is not enough to simply train hard, eat well, sleep well, etc. The power of the mind can be the one thing that can catch you out on the day. I have asked athletes to work with sports psychologists to cover all aspects of events and situations they may come across on race day, even if I have absolutely no concerns with how they themselves can perform in competition. The things that are worth discussing before they may (or may not) happen, are how you may deal with things like publicity, pressure of expectation of family, friends or the press, reactions of crowds, how you may feel if you become delayed, the stress of people within the support team around you and how that may affect you, issues with a coach, injury and even personal problems. Spending time planning means that the athlete is well prepared for any eventuality, and has the tools to be able to positively influence their reaction as circumstances change.

The Secret Behind Thought Processes:

Step back and think, "Is it true?" and then live 'as if.'

Fact Behind the Secret: - There is a direct correlation between your thoughts, feelings and behaviour which is fed by your perspective of any given situation.

There are a number of tools that are easy to master which can change your thought processes, your attitude, mood, confidence and mental state. Changing these will directly affect your performance. The first step is to become aware of these tools, the second is to put them into practice. This chapter shows you how.

"Thinking is not something that happens to you. It is something that you do."

What Were You Thinking?

Have you ever wondered why some days things work out really well, you train well, you are pleased with your progress, you feel happy and confident, but on other days the opposite happens?

In every event in our lives, big or small, we use all five of our senses to process things. This then allows us to form our version of what is going on. This will not necessarily be the same as someone else's version of the same event. For example, if you asked two gym users what their opinion of the gym was, there would undoubtedly be a difference in their description. One may feel it is too busy and hectic, another that they like the buzz of the place; and yet it is the same room.

Approaching things from different perspectives can change the picture completely.

What we see and experience influences our mood which ultimately influences our behaviour.

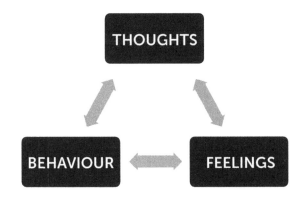

This is a three way process with each aspect influencing the other.

Just imagine waking up in the morning and hearing the birds tweeting. You realise it sounds like a lovely summer's day. If your response to this is positive your thought process may be along the lines of, "What a great day, I can go for a run." However, your response to this could be very negative, "Oh no! It's a lovely day I have to go for a run." You can see here how your mood can influence your behaviour.

> *"You've got to get up every morning with determination if you're going to go to bed with satisfaction."*
>
> **George Horace Lorimer**

To demonstrate the link between your thoughts and feelings try this exercise.

It is not possible to have a feeling without a thought.

😦 Try to feel sad without a sad thought.

😃 Try to feel happy without a happy thought.

😮 Try to feel guilty without a guilty thought.

It's just not possible and so we see how they are so closely linked.

We are never going to stop all negative thoughts, but we can learn to alter our response and make these responses more realistic

Have you ever wondered why sometimes you respond to someone or a situation in a way you were not expecting? The reason behind this lies in the difference between our conscious and sub-conscious mind.

In this chapter you will learn the difference between the two. A better understanding of the way your mind works will give you as a sports person a better understanding of how to get the most out of yourself and your performance.

The Importance of Our Two Minds:

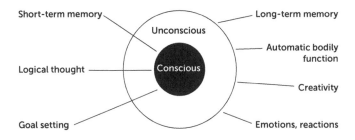

The conscious mind in sport is responsible for:

- setting your goals.
- arranging your training.
- deciding on tactics.
- analysing what parts of your game need improving.

The conscious mind is where we find logical thought. It holds your short-term memory and it is what you use to go about your day.

There are frequent times in sport when you have to logically analyse exactly what you need to do to perform in your chosen sport. There are also times when your unconscious mind takes over. For example, a tennis player relies on his subconscious mind to react to a ball that is coming towards him at over 100kph. The unconscious mind is running your body at this very moment. You are not concentrating on blinking; you are breathing and the unconscious is sorting out your blood sugar levels right now. When you are asleep you continue to breathe, but you are unaware of all of this at a conscious level.

⚿ The unconscious mind is very powerful and has huge capacity. It is responsible for:

- your long-term memory which includes every situation you have been in.

- every emotion you have felt.

- every reaction to a person or event.

- every practice session you have done.

- every time you have hit a ball, swum a length, bowled a ball, run a race.

This also explains why some reactions are not understood because if you have been in that situation or a similar one before, your subconscious will react as it did before because it has not been told to do anything different.

A little while ago I was introduced to a man called Roger and found myself taking an instant dislike to him. This puzzled me as I pride myself on getting on with most people. A little while later I was thinking about this encounter and realised that way back in secondary school I had been badly treated and embarrassed by a boy called Roger. The memory and reaction were still affecting me in adulthood.

The unconscious mind follows instructions. Therefore, if you are a golfer and you three putt on the green muttering "I am terrible at putting", then guess what? The unconscious mind does what it is told and you are now officially terrible at putting!

The more positive way of looking at this is that the unconscious mind can allow you to break through barriers that had previously been put in place. Back in May 1954, Roger Bannister fully believed he would break the four minute mile which most people believed was not possible. His philosophy was "Psychology and other factors set the razor's edge of defeat or victory."

⚬━ How to Make the Unconscious Mind Work to Improve Your Performance:

The unconscious mind needs simple instructions. It will follow orders, but will respond better to the use of your five senses. This is why visualisation is so effective. For example you could be lined up at the start of a race and say to yourself, "Focused and fast." This is a short, simple direction that the subconscious can follow. Add to this a visualisation of the feeling you get when running fast with the sound that accompanies this and you will have given very clear instructions. We will look at visualisation in detail in a separate chapter.

The unconscious mind needs practice. If, for example, you practise your swimming race start again and again, once you have set yourself in position, the subconscious mind takes over. Whenever a sports person feels that their body is just flowing perfectly, the subconscious has been allowed to take over. The subconscious will always perform as it has been taught. Be warned though that if you constantly practise missing a penalty, then that is what you will get!

Do you remember when you first started to learn to drive? To begin with you had a lot to learn, but with plenty of practice you passed your test. Are there ever times now, when you get to your destination and can't really remember the drive there? The reason for this is that you have repeated the same actions so many times that your subconscious knows exactly what it is expected to do.

With clear instructions and enough practice, your subconscious becomes a great tool to help you reach peak performance.

What your subconscious needs is clear instructions.

Include your senses when visualising.

Your purpose must be positive.

What you practise is what you will get.

When you are performing at peak performance and your body is doing exactly what you want it to do almost on autopilot, your subconscious mind has taken over. Imagine that you are writing an instruction manual for your subconscious so that it knows exactly what it is that you require of it.

Some ideas could be to think about:

- what is it you want that will specifically improve your performance?

- what would it feel like to train/compete as if on autopilot?

- how would your body respond?

- which parts of your performance would flow better?

- what would other people see when they watched you?

Now, sitting quietly, close your eyes, take two deep breaths that you hold for a few seconds before releasing the breath and relaxing. Whilst sitting there think about the things you have just decided would be helpful to you and run them through in your mind, bringing in as many senses as possible. For example, if you are imagining the perfect training run when your subconscious takes over and just allows your body to perform well, include what your feet would sound like as you ran. What is it that you would see? If you can include the taste and smell senses, then this becomes even more effective.

> "Our subconscious minds have no sense of humour, play no jokes and cannot tell the difference between reality or an imagined thought or image. What we continually think about will eventually manifest itself in our lives." Robert Collier

Is it True?

Sometimes your thoughts and feelings can affect your behaviour in such a way that is it unhelpful for your goal. For example, if you have an argument with your coach because you feel he doesn't think you are working hard enough, it could leave you feeling miserable, fed up and your enthusiasm for training may be affected. There is a very useful process that can help you to look at this situation.

Ask yourself, 'Is it true?'

Sometimes stepping back and really looking at the situation can change your perspective, which will ultimately change your behaviour.

Let's put this into an easy to follow table.

What has happened?	What thoughts are going through your head?	How you feel about it?	What other possible conclusions can you draw? Is it true? (Brainstorm as many possible solutions as you can think of)	How do you feel now?
Argument with coach	What's the point? I know I am working hard. What does he expect of me? He's being unfair. He doesn't treat the others like that.	Fed up Annoyed Frustrated	Perhaps I was a little lazy. Maybe he expects more of me than others as he sees more potential in me. It could be nothing to do with me. He may be affected by something else. It's up to me how I respond. I am en route to my goal, I need to refocus. Perhaps he felt I needed a shake-up. He is on my side.	Re-motivated Happier Focused

This process will allow you to change your reactions to situations that had previously left you feeling, and possibly behaving, in a negative way.

The time to use this tool is when you become aware of a shift in your feelings or thoughts. For example, when you walk into a room full of people who are all deep in discussion, and when they see you the room goes quiet. If you imagine this scenario you will also notice how it affects your feelings.

Activity:

This is an extremely useful and powerful tool to help you reassess a situation.

Remember, opinions are not facts

Think of a situation you have been in recently that you could apply this process to and fill in the table below. It could be a competition that has not gone exactly to plan or maybe a training session that left you feeling despondent.

When you fill in the column 'Is it True?' brainstorm as many different things as you can possibly think of, even if they don't appear to be relevant. It can be surprising what insight comes from what appears to be irrelevant.

What is the situation?	How you feel about it?	What other possible conclusions can you draw? Is it true?	How are you feeling /thinking now?

⚿ Act 'As if:'

One of the most important and easiest ways to improve your performance is to stay positive. This is sometimes easier to say than to do, but it is easy to alter your thoughts and feelings simply by acting 'as if.'

We have seen that looking at a situation from a different perspective can change the way you feel, think and behave. But what would happen if we attacked this from a completely different angle? What if your whole body language, tone, words and actions are in line with how you want to behave?

Here's an experiment for you to try.

Get together with a friend and stand still with your friend behind you.

Raise your dominant arm and ask your friend to try to push it down whilst you resist (gently, so you don't injure yourself).

Return your arm to your side and say out loud, "I am weak and feeble." Say this ten times with real conviction.

Raise your arm and ask your friend to push it down. This should happen very easily now.

Return your arm to the side and repeat the process, but this time saying, "I am strong and powerful."

Your friend should have difficulty moving your arm down.

This shows the power of your self-talk.

🗝 Notice the way that you speak to yourself within your own chatterbox. Speak positively and your attitude will follow.

The mind can have a profound effect on you physically which is why it is so important to work on it alongside your physical training.

"There are two ways to live: you can live as if nothing is a miracle; you can live as if everything is a miracle."
Albert Einstein

🗝 Holding your nerve to take a penalty, to sink a putt on the eighteenth green, to hold the line in a bike race, or to serve well on match point, all require your thoughts and feelings to be fully controlled. This then allows your subconscious mind to take over and do what it has been told and what it has practised.

Conclusion:

All thoughts, feelings and behaviours are interlinked. Your subconscious takes over when you are at peak performance. Tell it what you want using its rules.

Ask yourself, "Is it true?" when you notice a reaction you would rather change.

Live 'as if' you were achieving everything you have set your sights on.

Everybody's perception of a situation, event, place or person will be different.

⚓ Time to Reflect and Put a Plan of Action in Place:

- What has been your biggest learning from this chapter?
- Select at least two tools which you are going to start using from this chapter and write them down.

1.

2.

- How and when are you going to start using them?
- How will this improve your performance?

CHAPTER TWO:

FOCUS

Alistair Patrick Heselton – British Paralympic 7-a-side footballer.

Alistair's Story and His Use of Focus:

In the time leading up to September 10th 2006, I had been playing as a semi-pro footballer whilst training to become a chartered quantity surveyor in London's West End. Prior to that, I had been a young professional footballer at Queen's Park Rangers and during my time there I had enjoyed a great loan period at Oldham Athletic.

On the 10th of September 2006, I was the passenger in a tragic car accident which left one friend dead and another critically injured. I suffered severe head trauma (compound depressed fractured skull) which led to two brain haemorrhages. I was in a coma for several weeks.

After coming through that ordeal I had been told by doctors that I should never play football again, as any form of contact to my head should be avoided (this was after doctors initially telling my parents that I may be left in a vegetative state).

It was fairly clear early on that this would not be the case. However, I did not return to my normal self. After coming to terms with the reality of not playing football again I came to a decision, no matter what I could or couldn't do with my life, I would make sure that I would live to the highest standard that I was able to.

For me, this did mean I was able to go to the gym and keep myself as fit as possible in a recreational manner so I could take pride in myself. In life, I had always wanted to be successful in whatever I did and one day wanted to be married and have children. With that in mind, I continued to stay active and healthy so I would one day be able to do all of those things to the best of my ability. I applied the same goal settings I use in any sport. I would track my progress in how I looked and set myself weight targets with achievement dates.

Had I not done these things, my life to an extent would have been pointless and more of a struggle, as living from day to day would have meant that I was always reacting to what was before me rather than moulding my own future. By setting goals to aim for, it meant my life was spent going through the process of achieving them, which gave me a structure and discipline.

For inspiration I would often look back at the medals and trophies I had won, remembering what they were for and the feelings they gave me. That is something I still do today and I relive those moments before matches.

After falling in love with football again and proving to myself I was still able to compete at a high level, I went on to make my England debut at the CPISRA World Championships, scoring on my debut and also another in the second match I played.

I went on to represent Paralympics GB at London 2012, contributing with three assists and scoring in the play-off game against Argentina. I now aim to continue playing for England at the European and World Championships with the aim of being able to be selected for the Paralympic Games in Rio 2016.

Alistair's Sporting Success Tip:

I know exactly how powerful the mind is. Without having the right focus I would not have made it to the Paralympics. Your focus will change. Initially, my focus after the crash was just surviving. Then my focus changed once I was given the hope of playing again. With the right mindset I have been able to channel my thoughts, actions and beliefs in creating the success and joy that I currently have in my life.

I believe your overall focus should be spread over two key areas. Firstly, an overall goal and secondly, setting process goals.

For example:

1) **My Overall Goal:** Be selected for the Rio 2016 Paralympic Games 7-a-side football team. This is a long-term ultimate ambition which can only be achieved by fulfilling my process goals.

2) **Process Goals to Make My Overall Goal Possible:** To do this I would need to be playing well at international level for England at the European and World Championships, as well as having successful selection camps.

These can be broken down further still on a day-to-day basis. I must attend my gym training and technical football sessions in order to keep my body and mind focused. Before you know it, habit keeps you going.

"My time is always now, my time is always here. I just have to keep my body focused and my MIND in gear!"

The Secret Behind Focus:

You are only truly focused if you are completely in the present moment.

Science Behind the Secret:

Researchers at the Kavli Institute for Systems Neuroscience and Centre for the Biology of Memory at the Norwegian University of Science and Technology (NTNU Nov 19 2009) have discovered a mechanism that the brain uses to filter out distracting thoughts, allowing you to focus on a single piece of information. Just like radio stations play songs and news on different frequencies, the brain uses different frequencies of waves to send different kinds of information. Information is carried on top of gamma waves, just like songs are carried by radio waves. These carrier waves transmit information from one brain region to another. There are slow gamma waves and fast gamma waves coming from different brain areas, just like radio stations transmitting on higher or lower frequencies.

The lower frequencies are used to transmit memories of past experiences, and the higher frequencies are used to convey what is happening where you are right now. If you think of the example of the jammed radio, the way to hear what you want out of the messy signals would be to listen really hard for the latest news while trying to filter out the unwanted music. The hippocampus part of the brain does this more efficiently. It simply tunes in to the right frequency to get the station it wants. As the cells tune into the station they're after, they are actually able to filter out the other station at the same time, because its signal is being transmitted on a different frequency.

The cells can rapidly switch their activity to tune in to the slow waves or the fast waves, but it seems as though they cannot listen to both at the exact same time. This is like when you are listening to your radio and you tune in to a frequency that is midway between two stations. You can't understand anything. It's just noise.

Once we begin to focus on the present moment and take greater control of our thoughts, the mind begins to clear and the jammed radio station is able to tune into the exact station it wants to listen to. Your brain is able to focus, as it's not being confused by past thoughts or feelings and is in fact allowed to become a clear and focused channel.

Unlocking Your Secret:

🔑 In many contexts, connecting to your focus means tuning in to and trusting your body, connecting to the step/stroke/shot/swing in front of you. This is simply about being present. As soon as we start letting in thoughts of the past or the future, our focus is taken away from us. When we are truly focused, only the present moment counts.

🔑 Remember, you have control of your thoughts. It is your choice which radio station you want to tune in to. You can select the "Crazy Radio Station" full of unhelpful thoughts and distracting noise or the "Successful Radio Station" based on truth, clarity and focus.

Example: There is a story about a golfer who started planning his winning speech on the seventeenth hole. Guess what? By the end of the eighteenth hole he never got to make his winning speech! He let his mind wander to the future and had forced his focus to leave him. Instead of being present and playing shot by shot, his mind shut down as it thought he had finished performing.

"The successful warrior is the average man with laser-like focus."

Bruce Lee

What Does Focus Look and Feel Like?

Why does this photograph make you think the swimmer is focused?

1.

2.

Create Your Own Focus Photograph:

🔑 To create your own photograph of focus, we need to look back at some of your past performances and identify if you have any different thought patterns or processes.

- Write down an example of one your best performances.

- Where and when did this performance take place?

Think back to this event and create a clear picture in your mind of this performance. Think back to what you were doing **before**, **during** and **after** you competed.

Please fill out the charts below so we can uncover your peak performance state and learn how you can take greater control of this and create more consistency in your performances.

Best Performance:

	BEFORE THE COMPETITION	**DURING** THE COMPETITION	**AFTER** THE COMPETITION
THINKING	e.g. Focusing on what I wanted to happen	e.g. Strategy and technique	e.g. Proud of performance
FEELING	e.g. Prepared, focused	e.g. Strong	e.g. Happy
ACTING	e.g. Chatty, confident body language	e.g. Confident	e.g. Energised

Worst Performance:

As you've learnt, the more we focus on the positive the more we increase our confidence levels. However, at times it is useful to reflect on negative performances, as long as we recognize 'learnings' and use these to create a plan of action. In this exercise we are contrasting your best performance to your worst performance.

- Write down an example of one of your worst performances.

- Where and when did this performance take place?

- Think back to this event and create a clear picture in your head of this performance as you think back to what you were doing before, during and after you competed.

	BEFORE THE COMPETITION	DURING THE COMPETITION	AFTER THE COMPETITION
THINKING	e.g. Not sure I can do this	e.g. What other people will be thinking about me	e.g. I let everyone down
FEELING	e.g. Nervous	e.g. Frustrated	e.g. Upset and disappointed
ACTING	e.g. Unfocused and fearful body language	e.g. Rushing	e.g. Angry

⊶ Unlocking Your Peak Performance State

- What are the main differences in the BEFORE column between both performances?

- Is your focus better when things are not going your way or when they are?

- If you lose focus, how quickly can you regain fully connected focus?

- What things can you control in your best performance state?

- What are your two key words or phrases from your best performance state?

- How can you use your best performance state chart to help you prepare before competitions to help you have greater focus?

- When you are focused what are your key thoughts, feelings and actions?

- What do you know now that you didn't know before you completed this exercise?

Time to Play!

As we move through this book, you will start to realise how your mind can play tricks on you. This is a chance to start playing tricks on your mind! The secret is to take greater control over what you choose to focus on. If you fully engage in the exercises and activities in this book, you will have unlocked some tools to help you take greater control of your mind and increase your focus.

So let's start to play with some of these tools:

🔑 Focusing Yourself:

A calm mind gives the clearest focus.

An effective way to control heart rate and focus on the present is to learn to use some simple relaxation exercises. We have included a number of relaxation techniques in the Mental Imagery chapter. Here we will look at a quick and easy breathing technique which involves a deep and long inhalation of air into the diaphragm. Inhaling air into the diaphragm is a biological tool that helps control the heart rate and enables the athlete to have greater focus.

Exercise:

Option 1: Find a quiet place, shut your eyes and breathe in for six seconds, hold for two and breathe out for seven seconds. Repeat this three times.

Option 2: After you breathe in, simply say the word "focus."

Option 3: Press the 'slow' button. Slow your breathing, your actions and motions. Choose one instruction from your many practice sessions and concentrate on only that until your focus is back in place.

Experiment:

Play with this technique and take note of when it would be most useful for you. For example, if you make a bad shot and you want to regain your focus.

Practise Focusing:

Like anything in life, if you practise you will get better at it, and focusing is no different.

Try having a conversation with somebody and really listening to what they are saying until all other noises and distractions no longer exist for you.

Another idea is to really concentrate and focus on the word **FOCUS**. Look at it until it stands out from the rest of the text on this page.

These skills can then be transferred to the training ground and competition. With practice, you will find it easier to focus solely on the task in hand, to the exclusion of all other distractions around you.

○━ᴦ Focus Statement:

Imagine you are about to compete in the biggest competition of your life, and the best coach you have ever had is standing next to you. Sixty seconds before the competition begins, your coach looks you in the eye and tells you that if you stayed focused on this one thing or two things, you will be successful today.

What one or two things would the coach name? Be as specific as possible and remember to avoid using the word "don't." Focus instead on the things you want to happen, e.g. a smooth, confident shot.

🔑 Creating Your Own Video:

In this scenario, instead of watching a video of yourself performing, you are going to generate video clips of yourself in your head. This tool is based on mental imagery. For a more detailed overview of visualisation please refer to the Mental Imagery chapter. Visualisation is the act of watching something in your own mind, almost like a controlled daydream. Once again, it is something very simple, but it is an exceptionally powerful tool.

"I use a number of these visualisation techniques as a key part of my training. I have definitely noticed that it provides me with greater success"

Tyrone Swaray – International 100m sprinter

🔑 Your Video

- Part one – Find a quiet place, shut your eyes and take three deep breathes to calm and focus your mind. Now think back to a successful past performance and, for about a minute, run through this performance in your head. Put yourself back into the performance and make your past performance feel real again. Notice how you feel, what you are saying to yourself and what you were thinking.

- After about sixty seconds, hit the pause button on what you consider to be your greatest moment in your sport to date. Hold this image in your head for about thirty seconds. Savour this moment. Let in how proud you feel and how happy you look.

- Part two – Now picture yourself hitting the fast forward button as you see yourself competing at a future competition. From the things you have learnt in this chapter, which you now know help you with your focus, notice what you can control, how you are feeling, what you are saying to yourself and the success this is creating.

Conclusion:

When you are performing, this is the time to stop assessing and reassessing. It is the time to fully focus and let your mind and body do what it has trained and practised doing. It is about being truly present and being in the 'now'. We have provided a number of techniques for you to play with so that you can create greater focus and find the right tools that work for you.

Whilst playing with these new tools, we suggest you set up some time to evaluate your progress which should take you about five minutes. After each performance, take time to reflect and answer the following questions:

O— Evaluation after Training/Competing:

- What did I do well?

- What would I do differently?

- Where was my focus and where do I want it to be?

- When and why was I more focused?

- How can I improve on my focus tomorrow?

Keep it simple. Practise using your new tools and reflect on how the changes are improving your focus. In doing this, it will naturally bring you greater success.

⚷ Time to Reflect and Put a Plan of Action in Place:

- What has been your biggest learning from this chapter?

- Select at least two tools which you are going to start using from this chapter and write them down in your log book.

1.

2.

- How and when are you going to start using them?
- How will this improve your performance?

CHAPTER THREE:

CONFIDENCE

Sheree Cox, ISSF rifle shooter.

2008 - Youth Commonwealth Games gold in ladies 3x20 rifle event and bronze in ladies prone rifle event (Pune, India)

2009 - Youth Olympic Festival silver in ladies 3x20 event (Sydney, Australia)

2010 - Part of England rifle team for the Delhi Commonwealth Games - Seventh place in air rifle pairs

2007 - 2013 Part of Team GB for World Cups and European Championships worldwide

2014 - Part of England rifle team for Glasgow Commonwealth Games - fifteenth in women's air rifle and sixteenth in ladies 3x20 event

Aiming towards the 2018 Commonwealth Games in Gold Coast, Australia.

Sheree's Views on Confidence:

Over the years of shooting, practising and watching others shoot and compete, you learn how to build up your own confidence. The first match I ever competed in, I was so nervous and shaking that I couldn't load the rifle with a bullet. Now the fact I can is where I take my first bit of confidence. Over the years and the many successes I have had is where I get my confidence from, but the real trick is to generate confidence from nothing. How do you go into a competition without any confidence and pump yourself up ready to go? For me, music is the key thing and not just any radio station or album on my phone, but music with no words, such as film theme tunes. Pirates of the Caribbean has brilliant fast paced music that can spur you on and get you in a good frame of mind to compete. Having no words to remember is key, as it means that you won't run to the rhythm of the song as much or put meaning behind the words. Also, whilst listening to inspirational music, I visualise myself shooting well and the feeling I might have behind it. Visualisation and meditation are key things I use to generate confidence for my shooting, especially during the half hour to an hour before the match itself. Use music or whichever way you choose, to zone in to your match/race time.

The thing I know now that I didn't as a junior is that there are times, no matter how hard you try, you will find it hard to generate confidence. Life and sporting careers have many ups and downs and when you have had a really bad match or race, it is very difficult to come back from it. But what I know now is that you can use the 'downs' to pump you up for the 'ups'. I let my mind explore the bad times. Don't be afraid to relive the feelings you had then, and use them to say, "You know what... I didn't like that feeling. I don't want to feel like that again," and ask yourself, "How and what is in my control to make sure that doesn't happen again?" Use the negative feelings to spur on the good feelings and go out there and try harder, give more and get back to where you want to be.

Sheree's Tip for Sporting Success:

Soak up everything. In sport you have to be a sponge and listen to everyone. It doesn't mean you have to take on all that advice or be coached by everyone, but there are some you should listen to. I keep a 'tip' book, so that if I hear a good idea, I write it down and use it the next time I want to try something new, or for times when nothing seems to work. It gives you something to work on.

Jamie Baulch once said he trained on Christmas Day, as he knew his fellow competitors wouldn't, so when he was on that race line, he knew he had trained at least one day more than his rivals.

I also have a red book. This is a book that no one ever reads as it is full of nonsense. If before your match or training session, something goes wrong or you are in an adverse situation, you can write it in the book and forget about it. Metaphorically, it is out of your head, allowing you to focus on the job in hand. It can be a name of someone, a situation, or something you have forgotten, etc. At first I thought it was a silly idea, but now it travels with me through any competition, whether it be domestic or international.

Most of all, enjoy every experience. Keep a note of all the places you have been and what facilities were at each venue, so you know next time and can be better prepared. Enjoy making new friends and competing at whatever level you can achieve and always go there to beat yourself. Every time you beat yourself on time, score or distance, it leads to you eventually getting the number one slot and enjoying hearing YOUR national anthem. My key motto is 'Fail to prepare, prepare to fail'. If you know you have put your all in, that will give you the confidence you need to win!

The Secret Behind Confidence:

The beliefs you hold and the thoughts you have are keys to either making you strong and empowered or weak and tense.

Science Behind the Confidence Secret:

As we've been discovering, the mind is extremely powerful. We've examined that, through your thought processes, if you think you are capable of achieving more, you feel positive and you become able to do more. This is also true with negativity. If you think of yourself as a failure, you will feel down and this is likely to lead to a less positive outcome.

We can relate this directly to creating and controlling confidence. Science backs up this theory. If you've heard of the placebo effect, you are aware that belief in itself is capable of healing the human body. Doctors have researched that by giving a dummy pill containing no medicine, it can have a positive physical effect on a patient's condition. The patients are not aware that it is a dummy pill, so psychologically they think they are taking medicine to help their condition. By simply having the belief that they will get better, they actually affect their own physiologies.

When you think of someone who you consider is confident, do you notice that they seem to project their personality outwards? And the people who lack confidence seem to go inwards and shrink. Body language plays a major role in how people perceive you and how confident you are. The way you hold yourself, your hand, eye and face movements are constantly giving off signals about the state of your mind.

The great thing is that you can take complete control of your body language and send nonverbal messages of confidence to those around you. This is not so much about faking it as behaving confidently which can rewire your beliefs and feelings. Science refers to this as the principle of retrospective rationality. Your brain likes to believe that you are behaving in a way that is consistent with your beliefs. So if you start behaving as a confident person, your brain forces your mind to believe you are a confident person.

Another interesting facet is that by behaving confidently you make others feel confident about you. Remember, people aren't mind readers and can't tell what is going on in your head, so even if you are feeling nervous, if you behave with confidence, people will believe you to be confident and treat you that way too.

Unlocking Your Secret:

O━ Remember, confidence is a quality that anyone can gain more of. You can always choose to take action and apply the skills from this chapter which will naturally increase your self-belief.

O━ Your mind can often play tricks. Be aware that you can also play tricks on your mind. Get ready to empower yourself and take greater control by learning some mind tricks!

Sasha Corbin, nineteen international caps. England netball player since 2009.

Sasha's View on Confidence:

First and foremost, I trust that everything I have done leading up to a competition or match has been done to the best of my ability. I am confident in my preparation and the test is the competition or match. Before I compete, I like to set myself a goal or two; something simple that I would like to execute well. This gives me focus and helps with my confidence.

When you believe in yourself, you can achieve your goals. People can believe in you, but it's up to you to believe in yourself. Talent only gets you so far. You really do have to train hard to be the best. Injuries really can make you stronger.

Sasha's Sporting Tip:

You have to push yourself in training to get to the next level. If you don't, you are only cheating yourself or your team. You play or compete the best when you're having fun, so enjoy it :)

Understanding Your Sources of Confidence:

In this chapter, we will examine a wide range of areas to help increase and control your confidence. Some aspects will be looking at improving your self-belief and others will involve building upon existing facts.

Whether we are working with an Olympic athlete or an amateur sportsperson, confidence is always something that can be improved upon. Firstly, we need to uncover what drives their internal self-belief and from here, various tools and techniques are applied to enable that athlete to have a specific routine, so that it becomes part of their preparation. This means that the athlete has greater control over their confidence.

Building your confidence is like assembling a jigsaw puzzle. We will help you gain a greater understanding of yourself in this chapter and provide you with the tools you need to naturally increase your confidence.

The Main Keys for This Chapter are:

O— Your mindset and beliefs

Confident athletes are positive and optimistic. As we've discussed, it is about being positive and realistic. Many athletes can beat themselves up for their mistakes. This then creates fear, leading to a lower level of confidence. Remember, we are not perfect. We are going to make mistakes at times, but it is about learning from these experiences and growing from them.

O— Your behaviour

Science proves, if you behave confidently, you can help rewire your brain to help you think more confidently and feel more confident about yourself.

O— Your goals

Confident athletes set goals. Please refer to our Goals chapter. Once you know what you want, it is a lot easier to make the right choices. You can get there a lot quicker by setting a goal.

O— Your resources

Confident athletes draw upon resources to help them develop and maintain their confidence. This might be through drawing on their support team, their environment and facts about their performances.

⚷ Your resilience

Confident athletes bounce back from setbacks. Even though you can't control everything that happens to you, you can always control your attitude and how you choose to respond. My ninety-five year old grandmother has a great motto which is KPO: Keep Powering On. When I look at her, she is the vision of resilience.

Having Fun with Confidence

Try having a conversation with two different approaches. When you do this, notice which makes you feel more confident and whether you have a different response from the other person.

1. Drop your head, look at the ground and cross your arms. Talk in a quiet, low and uninterested voice.

2. Stand tall, maintain eye contact, have your arms by your side or use your hands to express yourself. Talk clearly, confidently and with passion.

"If you think you can or you think you can't – you're right"

Henry Ford

How Does Confidence Look and Behave?

When you think of confidence, perhaps the first thing that comes to mind is how confident people behave. It is important to remember that how people come across is only a part of being confident. We need to grasp these skills and be aware of what confidence allows us to achieve. Confidence is mainly about enabling people to achieve their goals. This is because confident people focus on the following:

O—π They grasp new opportunities and see these as exciting new adventures.

O—π They cope with setbacks and take these as learnings.

O—π They take responsibility for themselves and for making the necessary changes to create greater success.

O—π They look at situations as opportunities rather than something fearful to be avoided.

O—π They push past negative emotions and setbacks in order to reach their goals.

O—π They know what they want and set goals to create a sense of purpose and direction.

O—π They take time to be grateful and reflect to boost their confidence.

As we can see from this list, there are a number of differences between confident and less confident people. It is not how much they feel anxiety, it is how they deal with the situations, regardless of their fears.

Confidence is about taking action however you may feel at the time. It is about doing what you need to do in the short-term to achieve your long-term goals. It is vital that you manage those feelings in order to achieve these long-term goals. This is another reason to set goals. If you haven't got a goal already, visit the Goal chapter and map them out.

Confidence is about taking action and taking control. It's time to put you back in the driving seat!

Rearrange this list, placing the items that give you the most confidence at the top and those that influence your confidence levels the least at the bottom.

- Past success in my sport
- An effective training programme
- Immediate performance
- Positive comments from others
- Supportive people in your life
- Training or quality practice
- Quality coaching
- Positive/optimistic coaching
- Belief in your physical talent
- Your method or technique
- The quality of your equipment
- Warm up routine
- Comfortable with environment
- Mental preparation
- Study and preparation
- Mental game coaching
- Coping well under pressure
- Good teamwork
- Positive rapport with coach
- Positive rapport with team
- Trust in teammates
- Sports diet
- Other sports you played
- Game plan or strategy

Rank Your Sources of Confidence:

From the list on the previous page insert your top 5 things that give you confidence and how you can control these.

My Top Things That Give Me Confidence are:	How Can I Control This:
e.g. Past success in my sport	I've written a list for the past three years of all my successes. The night before an event I am going to read through this list. As I warm up before a competition I am going to visualise these successes.
1.	
2.	
3.	
4.	
5.	

Old and New Beliefs:

We've identified that confidence is a mind game and once we understand this we can start learning how to take greater control and increase our self-belief. Confident people believe in themselves and because of this, they create opportunities which enable them to achieve. When we break this down, we realise how important our beliefs about ourselves are and how these relate to our performance.

If we look at your peak performance charts, (Focus chapter) examine what your beliefs and attitudes were before your best performance. You will then be able to identify what messages you were giving yourself. Did you fuel your confidence or drain it?

Whatever your current state of mind is, you can quickly improve your confidence by consciously changing the way you think about yourself and your performance.

1. What feelings do you associate with confidence?

2. When you think of confidence what does it look like?

3. When you feel confident what are you thinking?

Remember, if you think you are capable of achieving more, you feel upbeat, positive and you naturally achieve more. If you tell yourself you are likely to fail, you feel negative and worried, and guess what? You are likely to fail.

You are not born with your beliefs, attitude and thought processes. Your beliefs are influenced by what is going on around you, but more importantly by what you choose to believe!

For example: You are at a sporting event. You reach the finals and you are beaten. Different people can interpret situations very differently, even though the situation was identical.

One person may finish the match, get really angry and upset and fire their coach. Another person may assess their performance and take from it the positives, i.e. they made it to the finals, and also take away a number of learnings. Merely by approaching a situation with a different thought process, which person is likely to have a more solid belief system which will help generate greater confidence in the future?

It is evident that even though the situation was exactly the same, a thought process can result in two very different directions.

Now you are aware of this, in the table below, write down any old beliefs that you realise hold you back and limit you. In the column next to this, write down the new positive belief you are going to adopt.

Old Limiting Belief	New Beneficial Belief
1.	
2.	
3.	

Your Inner Coach:

Imagine you are interviewing two coaches and you are going to have to hire one of them. You ask both of them to give you thirty minutes of training.

Coach one: As you are getting ready to go out to train, she says to you, "Are you ready? Do you really think you are prepared enough to do this training today? You look tired and run down. I don't think you are going to perform well today."

Ten minutes into the training, you have been told the following by coach one:

"You are very slow and heavy on your feet."

"You will never make it to the next level."

"You don't have a solid technique."

Twenty minutes into your training, you make a few errors. Coach one comments:

"You should give up now and finish training today."

"Are you not angry with yourself because of your performance?"

You then take coach two out to training:

As you are getting ready to go out to train, coach two says to you:

"I'm looking forward to training today. My focus is that we work on things that will help you feel more focused and create greater confidence."

Ten minutes into the training, you have been told the following by coach two:

"You are working well and we are meeting your goals we set out prior to training."

"We can use this training to help you in your next competition."

"Your technique is solid and we can develop ways to continue your improvements."

Twenty minutes into your training, you make a few errors. Coach two comments:

"We have some good learnings we can put in place to strengthen your performance."

"Let's figure out what we can do differently in the future if this situation happened again."

So which coach would you hire?

This was an example to illustrate that you and what you actually say to yourself creates your inner coach. You would never hire a coach who was negative and made you feel awful before you even stepped out to training. However, have you ever done this to yourself? If you had to put up with this coach, he/she would grate on your nerves and destroy your self-confidence. We all have an inner voice, yet as we've seen, it can serve to help us or it can serve to limit us. Often we take more notice of the negative inner coach. Jump back into that driving seat and create and note what the positive coach tells you.

We have over one hundred thousand thoughts a day. You can see how your internal coach can influence the way you think and thus shape your beliefs.

Let's just do a quick inner coach check-in:

What are some positive things you say to yourself before competing/training?

How does this make you feel?

Is there a negative that you might sometimes say to yourself?

How does this make you feel?

What is the learning from this and how can you create an action plan to help you be a better inner coach to yourself?

Once again, we can back up the power of self-talk with science. Psychologist Michael Mahoney studied a group of gymnasts hoping to qualify for the US Olympic team. He questioned the gymnasts about their thoughts during competitions. He found the athletes that actually qualified for the Olympics had as many doubts and fears as the less successful ones. However, the successful athletes constantly encouraged themselves through positive self-talk. They illustrated the power of the inner coach and its impact. By telling yourself you can do it, you are more likely to create a positive outcome.

Find Your Best Coach in Yourself:

Think back to the last time you performed your best or revisit your peak performance chart. What was your self-talk like? What did you tell yourself and what were the positive statements you used?

Create four positive statements you can use to boost your confidence, e.g. "I can do this". "I can do anything I put my mind to." "Focus." "I'm prepared and ready."

1.

2.

3.

4.

Body Language:

Even if you are lacking in confidence, by changing your body language this has a direct impact on how you feel and how others perceive you. An added bonus to this, as if this isn't good enough already, your brain likes to believe you're behaving in a way that is consistent to your beliefs. So this means that if you start behaving in a confident way, your brain tries to explain your behaviour by forcing your mind to believe that you are a confident person. We saw this in the experiment we did at the beginning on how very slight shifts to your body language can alter someone's perception of you and also the perception you have of yourself.

"Don't fake it until you make it.
Fake it until you become it."

A Cuddy

Let's look at the animal kingdom as an example of body language.

When a cobra snake is under threat it opens itself up, making it appear larger, confident and dominant. This is a high power pose. When an animal is threatened, its body language shrinks and it appears fearful and unconfident. This is a low power pose.

Notice how this swimmer's celebratory open pose gives you the sense of the power and confidence he is feeling.

"Our subconscious minds have no sense of humour, play no jokes and cannot tell the difference between reality or an imagined thought or image. What we continually think about will eventually manifest itself in our lives." Robert Collier

As we will see throughout this book, it's about keeping things simple yet highly effective. One of the simplest techniques we use with clients is a very basic breathing technique. As we've seen, our minds and our bodies are completely connected. **Wherever the mind goes the body will follow**. This is evident in this next exercise. When we want to behave confidently, we have to appear confident. This exercise actually alters your physical state and can enable your mind to feel more confident.

When we are stressed, we take short, fast and shallow breaths, but by consciously being more aware of our breathing, we can encourage our minds to be more confident. When we focus on our breathing, it is possible to stop thoughts coming into our head. This enables us to be completely present and mindful. So let's get going with this simple belly breathing exercise.

1. Place your left hand on your chest and your right hand on your belly. Take a few short sniffs as though you are trying to smell something. You should feel your left hand moving.

2. Now take some long slow deep breaths into your belly. You should notice only your right hand rises and falls as you breathe.

3. Simply continue taking long deep breaths, focusing on your belly. Notice how calm and relaxed you feel.

Once you are comfortable with knowing your breathing is being directed to your belly, you can do this without using your hands. This exercise can be used at any time you need to feel more calm or confident.

What are the three changes you are going to make to your body language to help you feel, behave and look more confident?

1.

2.

3.

Perfection versus Confidence:

When people aim for perfection and their expectations are so high, they actually start limiting their own confidence. This is a problem we see regularly when working with athletes. We are not saying it is wrong to aim for perfection as it can act to stimulate motivation. However, there is a tipping point and if this is not balanced the athlete's self esteem can be limited as they are not creating a positive reality for themselves.

When we look at perfection, it is important to realise that it basically does not exist in anything. Think about your sport. Do you know for example any golfer, tennis player, hockey player or badminton player who has a perfect game? It is all about creating this balance to fuel your confidence. It's about being positive and **realistic**, reviewing performances and then giving ourselves a pat on the back.

Below is a chart. Look at the perfectionist qualities and tick the traits that sound similar to you personally. We all have some of these traits and some people have all of them. Remember, this is an exercise to achieve a sense of balance. The confidence column gives you an alternative behaviour.

Perfectionist	Confidence
1. High or strict expectations	1. Replace with manageable mini goals
2. Dwell on shortcomings	2. Focus on strengths
3. Fretting over past mistakes	3. Refocus on present
4. Self critical behaviour	4. Positive self-talk
5. Over analysis	5. Clear, focused mind
6. Easily frustrated	6. Let go of mistakes
7. Focus on future performance	7. Focus in the present

Drawing on Resources:

It is so important to surround yourself with like-minded people who support and genuinely care for you. Sometimes we have people in our lives that may not be good for our confidence. If you surround yourself with positive people, you will naturally feel more confident. We have an analogy for this. We refer to these positive people as radiators. These are the people who make you feel comfortable, at ease, and you want to spend time near them.

The other set of people we refer to as drains. They literally drain the energy away from you. They offer very little support and often just moan and talk negatively about other people.

It is important to realise certain people do not necessarily have your best interests at heart. They can often be jealous and can undermine your confidence, draining your enthusiasm. It is important to identify these people in your life and then choose the action you want to take. Either cut down the time you spend with them or completely cut them out of your life.

Other people can have a great deal of influence. Once you identify the radiators in your life, you can work at surrounding yourself with more like-minded people. People you feel comfortable with.

MY RADIATORS (The people who support me and bring out the best in me)	MY DRAINS (The people who drain me and have a negative influence)	ACTION TO BE TAKEN (increase or decrease time spent with them, communicate with them about this or cut them out of my life)

"Yesterday is history, tomorrow is a mystery, today is a gift, which is why we call it the present."

Bill Keane

Being more present is a great skill to embrace. In sport, this can help us dramatically when we get in the zone, but it will also help us become more relaxed and focused at the same time. By slowing down, reducing your thoughts and being more present, you can break the negative cycles such as worry, regret, anxiety, etc. and create a more positive existence for yourself.

Dealing with Setbacks:

In every setback there lies a lesson and an opportunity. The key to this is having the right attitude to identify the opportunity.

> *"There is no such thing as failure, only feedback."*
>
> **R Allen**

Have you noticed that confident people don't let setbacks get the better of them? We are human; we will all experience rejection and setbacks in our life. Confident athletes will at times get knocked down again and again, yet they will get up again and again. The key is to take on board the learnings and move forward.

Let's create building blocks to grow from, rather than road blocks that will stop you from moving forward.

You can't always control a situation, but you can always control how you respond to that situation. You can either choose to use it as an excuse to give up or as an opportunity to learn and carry on.

When you are stressed and you feel it might impact your confidence, there are a few simple questions you can ask yourself to get yourself back on track.

1. Rate it: How big a deal is this situation? Often when we are stressed we can blow things out of proportion. Take a reality check. Is anyone's life in danger? Is the world going to end? Rate the situation out of ten, with ten being a very big deal.

2. Time scale: Fast-forward six months and ask yourself how much of an issue will this be then. Often at the time, a situation can seem a lot worse. When we actually move on from the situation and look back we realise that in the grand scheme of things it was not worth stressing over.

3. Reaction: Has your reaction to the event been appropriate and effective? Is there a more effective way of dealing with the situation?

4. Take action: The situation has happened. Now it is time to consider if there is anything you could do to improve the situation. What action could you take to help?

5. Lesson: What have you learnt from this situation? How can you use this learning to help you in the future?

6. Help: What is one positive that you can pull from this situation?

MOVE ON. Roadblock removed and building block created.

When we look back at some of our setbacks in life, we actually realise they were blessings in disguise. It took Katie a while to realise her purpose and reason for her paralysis. It has been, and still is, a journey for her. In her own words, "I can honestly say, without that experience I would not be writing this book or have had the pleasure to have met and worked with so many wonderful people. My experience has directed me in my life. I became aware that my purpose was to help people."

As we've seen in this book, it is always important to take time to reflect. Let's look back at some of your setbacks and how they have become opportunities.

1. When looking back in your life, what do you now consider the best setback has been?

2. What happened to you?

3. At the time, why did you consider it to be a setback or a failure?

4. What do you know now about this situation? How has it helped you?

5. What has been your biggest learning from this?

When working with athletes, we are always on the search for simple solutions and ways to help people have greater clarity. The way to do this is to remove emotion from situations and get to the facts. Our mind can play tricks on us and the emotions can actually cover up the reality of the situation. Once you have the tools and the knowledge, you can cut through this, remove the emotion and find your building block.

Creating a confident future

As we've highlighted it is really important to review and keep track of your progress. We all need pats on the back and we need to monitor when we are moving closer to our goals. Without reassessing, we can start to go off road and it can all become harder than it needs to be. By reviewing you can readjust and try an alternate route to get you back on track.

It's time to revisit the goals section you completed. Remember every week to set yourself a mini goal so that you stay on track for your main goal.

My main goal is:

How am I moving closer to this? What progress have I made?

Is there anything at this stage that I need to tweak or change to help me stay on track?

When reviewing my goals and making any tweaks, how does this make me feel more confident?

Get Your Facts Together:

Another resource we can draw upon is reality; the facts. We often forget what we have achieved and can live too much in the future, focusing on what we want rather than what we actually have already.

So often your trophies and awards become ornaments rather than tools to help your confidence. It is important that you remind yourself of the reality you have created.

1. Pull together your awards and write down the memories from that day. What was it that helped you create the success and win that award?

2. Write down five things your coach/support team/friends have said to you that made you feel positive about yourself?

3. What is the thing you feel most proud of that you have achieved?

4. My strengths as an athlete are:

5. My top three sporting successes are:

6. The thing about my training preparation which gives me confidence is:

7. The thing that a person complimented me about my performance is:

8. My coach makes me feel confident when he says:

Communication:

It is important to consider if there are certain people you need to communicate with to talk through how they might increase or decrease your confidence.

As you've learnt to perform at your peak potential, it is vital to maximise your strengths to create a positive, focused and decisive mindset which generates confidence and consistency. By changing the way you use your mind, when you approach your sport, you will naturally improve your performance outcome.

The following are some tips to help you improve your mindset by taking greater control of your attitude, communication, confidence and preparation techniques.

1. Remember we are always learning.

2. Work together with your support team to keep a positive mindset.

3. Remove emotions and work with facts.

4. Ask questions if you don't understand something.

5. Remember that your support team are not mind readers.

6. Provide regular feedback to yourself and to your support team.

7. Be aware we all communicate in different ways.

8. Consider a situation from other peoples' points of view.

9. Be aware what someone says and what we hear can be very different.

10. Be grateful for everything your support team does for you.

11. Listen.

12. Create solutions.

We would suggest you also refer to the Communication chapter or review your answers to some of the exercises you have completed. People are not mind readers. Make sure you communicate how you feel and what you've learnt which will help you to create a plan together.

Preparation:

Proper preparation is the key to confidence. We refer to it as the five P's

• Proper Preparation Prevents Poor Performances

So let's examine your preparation and how we can build upon this to increase your confidence.

1. Why does preparation make you feel confident?

2. What is the most important part of your preparation routine, e.g. the night before having all my kit ready, mental preparation on the day, planning before a competition, etc.?

3. How can you control this part of your preparation?

4. What can you do to improve your preparation?

5. What is your action plan to make this improvement happen?

As we've discussed, mental rehearsal is an exceptionally powerful tool. This along with new scientific evidence shows how visualisation causes real chemical and physical changes in the brain and throughout the body. The brain doesn't distinguish between real and imaginary. When you imagine something, the brain believes it is really happening.

- Sit in a comfortable place where you are free from disturbances.

- Relax your body and take four long, slow breaths.

- See yourself training or competing with this new confidence you have discovered. What does it feel like and what do you look like? Has your body language changed? In what other ways have you developed more confidence and how is this making things easier and more enjoyable for you?

- Open your eyes and make a note of the changes you saw in your visualisation. Make sure you create an action plan to enable all of these positive changes to take place.

"What the mind can conceive, the mind can achieve."

Clement Stone

Conclusion:

Please remember we are human. We are not robots, and as long as we are making small steps forward, we are heading in the right direction. Remember, small changes make big differences. Be patient with yourself and enjoy the journey you are on. You never know what tomorrow holds. Make sure you make the most of each day and be grateful for what you have now.

It is so important to celebrate and give yourself a pat on the back when you deserve it. Be kind to yourself and avoid beating yourself up, as this directly impacts your confidence. Without giving yourself positive feedback, you may begin to take for granted and not recognise what you have achieved. Why limit yourself? Remember, you can always improve, yet whilst improving, take time to realise what you are achieving now. This will not only help your confidence, but you will feel more positive and enjoy life more.

⚲ Time to Reflect and Put a Plan of Action in Place:

- What has been your biggest learning from this chapter?

- Select at least two tools which you are going to start using from this chapter and write them down in your log book.

1.

2.

- How and when are you going to start using them?

- How will this improve your performance?

CHAPTER FOUR:

GOAL SETTING

Bryan Steele – four time Olympian winning both a silver
and a bronze medal.

Bryan's View on Setting Goals:

For the first ten years of my career, I didn't have a goal for
each year. This lead to under performance.

From 1988 I started to set long-term goals (Olympics cycle) and the goal for the coming session (this would be World Championships which would be the best marker for the Olympics).

With this goal I was able to focus towards it and having monthly goals, I tracked my progress.

This kept me focused and motivated, knowing that if I didn't achieve my shorter goals, then I would struggle to achieve my long-term goal.

Bryan's Sporting Success Tip:

Know where you would like to go in your sport. Dream and believe that anything is possible, but the main thing is that you are always learning and you can always do something better.

The Secret Behind Goal Setting:

You are more likely to get to where you want if you set a goal that is formed by knowing what drives you and then constantly review it.

Science Behind the Secret:

Goal setting has been very thoroughly researched. Locke & Latham found in 1990 (*A Theory of Goal Setting and Task Performance*) that specific, difficult and self-generated goals will benefit your performance more than not having a goal or setting one that is far too easy.

It is part of the human make-up to seek a goal. We feel comfortable when we have a clear direction. It gives us clarity.

Unlocking Your Secret:

It makes sense that if you know where you want to go and you can plan steps that will take you there, your motivation and focus will be greater than those who have no goal to reach.

Imagine a clear path to what you want to achieve, with each step laid out for you to concentrate on. Knowing exactly what it is you want and putting a plan into place to achieve it will increase focus and motivation.

Example: Michael Johnson, four time Olympic gold medallist recognised that his achievements were not based on pure talent. It was a combination of physical conditioning, mental strength, a clear vision of where he wanted to go and a plan of how to get there.

"A goal casually set and lightly undertaken will be freely abandoned at the first obstacle."

Zig Ziglar

Your Goal:

Setting a goal improves performance both mentally and physically. It allows you to concentrate your time and effort on a more specific target.

- Think about how often you look at setting a goal. How important is setting a goal to you? 0-10

0	1	2	3	4	5	6	7	8	9	10
Not important								Very important		

- **If you did not put down ten, then what can you do to make it a ten?**

To set a goal and make the process of goal setting more important to you, let's look at what benefits it will give you.

What a Goal Can Do for You:

- Pin-points exactly where you need to focus your attention.

- Increases your persistence as you have an end vision in mind.

- It can lead to a change in your attitude to training and performance.

- It increases your effort as you strive to achieve the goal.

- If you are focused on one direction, you are less likely to waste time and energy on irrelevant activities.

- If you are not moving towards a goal, where will you be six months from now?

- The whole point of goal setting is to facilitate success. Do you want to be successful?

Let's Build a

There are three types of long-term goals; performance, process and outcome.

Outcome Goal:

Winning the 100m butterfly at the Olympics is an example of an outcome goal. It relies not only on your performance, but also on the performance of the other competitors over which you have no control. Therefore, it is not the best type of goal. These are also called competitive or ego goals.

Process Goal:

Process goals focus on improving the actions or techniques that are required to achieve success. Examples of process goals would be improving your grip on a tennis racket, learning to control your breathing when running or training, or getting your pace right between hurdles.

When setting your goal, think about which part of your technique would ultimately help improve your performance.

A process goal relies solely on your effort and focus, and is therefore an excellent form of goal.

Performance Goal:

A goal such as running 400m in a certain time is a performance goal and relies solely on you. Performance goals, also known as mastery goals, focus on your overall performance.

In 1989 Nicholls, a renowned educational psychologist researched the difference between the effect on mastery of those who followed outcome based goals against those who followed mastery/performance/process driven goals.

In essence, he concluded that outcome goals led to a decrease in effort, enjoyment and performance, whereas those who followed process/mastery/performance goals increased their persistence, effort, motivation and enjoyment.

Therefore, to maintain motivation on your end goal, it is suggested that when you set a goal, it is better to make it a mastery/process/performance goal.

Positive Goals:

Your goal needs to be positive. A goal that states a negative will not be as effective. 'I don't want to fail' is negative and all you are telling the brain is what you don't want instead of what it is that you do want. A positive would be 'I will make every training session and focus for every minute of it.' When you read this statement it is clear exactly what you want to achieve.

Make it clear and make it positive.

To create an effective goal, follow each of the following sections and lets aim for the TARGET.

Time

Assess

Realistic

Gain

Explicit

Task

TIME

The first thing that needs to be looked at is the target date you want to set for yourself. When you have decided what this is, make sure you have given yourself enough time to achieve the target. Now let's break this down into manageable steps.

Imagine that you decide to set your goal for an event that is a year away from now. The next step would be to ask yourself, "What will I have to achieve six months, three months, one month, one week from now to reach that target?"

Write down how many days there are between now and your target date. This is your long-term target. Now break this down into mid and short-term dates.

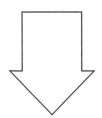

Long-Term Target:

Choose a specific date / event:

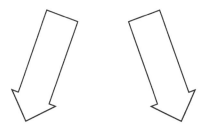

Mid-term Targets:

Choose a specific date between now and the long-term target date. You can have any number of these mid-term targets.

Now ask yourself what you need to do this week, today or now to start to move towards your target.

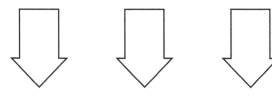

Short-term Targets:

These can be weekly or even daily targets.

ASSESS

Continually re-assessing allows you to track your progress. The easiest way to set a target that can be re-assessed regularly is to use numbers. For example, 'I will do ten reps' or 'I will train for forty-five minutes'.

Regular re-assessment is crucial in the target setting process, as without it, you will not be aware of the progress you are making and whether your target needs modification. It allows for feedback to be received from your training partner, team mates, coach or parents.

With any journey, you gain new knowledge and insight along the way. Assessing your progress allows you to adapt if necessary and also gives you the opportunity to congratulate yourself on the progress you have made; progress you may not have made if you had not set yourself a target.

If you include a feedback section in your training log, re-assessment will be on-going. A simple adjustment to your training log will allow you to write down your assessment and feedback. This can act as a tool for you to review the whole process when you get to your final target.

o—⚓ Many top performers use their training log books to review what targets they have met and monitor their training and focus, leading up to best and less than best performances. This speeds up their learning. Adding an element of assessment and feedback is a simple process that can benefit you enormously.

Date	Training	Specifics – time, weights, reps, distance, hours	Evaluation (What did I do well? What would I do differently?)
Monday	Ran	Time distance	Reduced time by ...
Tuesday	Gym	Number of reps	Confidence building
Wednesday	Swam	Distance	Increased focus
Thursday	Practised skills	Number of reps	More accurate
Friday	Sprinted	Time	Positive attitude
Saturday	Day off	Practised visualisation	Finding it easier
Sunday			
Feedback for the week. How am I better this week than last week?			How has this week's training moved me towards my goal?

If you don't use a log then ask yourself the following:

- How often will I reassess what progress I have made?
- How will I get feedback?
- Who do I want to give me feedback?
- Once I have feedback how I will readjust my target?

Part of assessment is reviewing your progress at the end of this process. What do you do if you have not achieved what you set out to achieve? This can happen. It even happens to those at the top of their game. This is the perfect time to re-assess. Did you set enough short-term goals? Did you look back on your progress at regular intervals? Was the target realistic? What have you learnt from this?

REALISTIC

If your target is unrealistic, you will fail to hit it. It would be unrealistic for a golfer with a handicap of twenty-five to expect to hit a target of a handicap of fifteen a month from now. You are setting yourself up for failure.

To be realistic, a target must aim at an objective towards which you are both willing and able to work. This is a good time to take an ecology check of your situation.

Here are some questions to ask yourself:

- How much time can you realistically give to this?
- Is the target and the process of reaching it sufficiently important to you?
- What is likely to get in your way?
- Can you really visualise yourself reaching this target?
- Are you ready to commit to the target? Is this goal important to those around you or just to you?

Realising you have a choice can lead to greater commitment to your chosen target.

GAIN

🔑 One of the main differences between people who achieve their goal and those who don't is the recognition of the motivation behind the goal.

One way you can make a target and the process of target setting more important to you is to look at what benefits it will give you. For a long-term goal to succeed, you need to find your passion. What is it that drives you? Perhaps this exercise will help you find your motivation.

Before filling in this table, think about the following:

What will you gain?

What will it mean to you to achieve this goal?

How will it change your life?

How will it change your performance?

How will you feel about yourself?

How will you be treated by those around you?

What will your coach notice?

Describe what life will be like for you one year from now if you do not set and achieve your target goal.	Describe what it will be like if you achieve your target goal.

Has this helped you discover what drives you?

Another way to discover your passion is to look at what has gone before. When you look at the targets you have set yourself and achieved in the past, ask yourself why they were so important to you that you stuck with them until you reached them. Really take some time to decide why you want this.

Try this simple but effective exercise devised by renowned goal setting expert Brian Tracy.

What do you want to achieve this year?

1 .... 2 ....

3 .... 4 ....

5 .... 6 ....

7 .... 8 ....

9 .... 10 ....

Now choose ONE that would have the biggest impact on your life if you could achieve it in the next twenty-four hours. This then becomes your focus which can be broken down into smaller steps. By setting yourself one thing every day it moves you towards that ultimate target.

Can you imagine reaching this target? If you can't, read the chapter on Mental Imagery to learn how to do this. Remember that the reality will not necessarily be an exact match to what you visualise, but the point is that your vision will give you a clear path, allowing you to make daily decisions which will in turn keep you moving towards your target goal.

EXPLICIT

If your target is explicit, it will be very clear to you what you need to do for each step to achieve that goal. This will give you clarity. Murky directions will only lead to confusion and make focusing more difficult. Clarity doesn't come to you. It is not a passive process. You have to make clear decisions and then commit to them in writing; a contract with yourself.

There are a number of questions that can help you give your target clarity.

- Who is involved?
- What is it that I want to achieve?
- Is there a certain location involved?
- Is there a time frame involved?
- What steps do I need to take to get there?
- What are the specific reasons I have chosen this target?
- How will I know when I have got there?

TASK

One of the most important characteristics of goal setting is getting the level of task and challenge just right. It needs to challenge you, but must be something you can obtain. Easy goals result in weak motivation, whereas goals that are too difficult result in disappointment. Setting an unattainable goal could be more de-motivating than setting a goal that is too easy. Find your level with enough challenge.

Being aware of your strengths and weaknesses will help you define the right level of challenge. Take a few moments to list them. Ask your coach to help if you find this difficult.

My strengths	My weaknesses

When you look at the task you have set, ask yourself, "Is it achievable? Can I do it if I focus? Is it within my capabilities?"

There are certain things in life that are not in our control and this has to be taken into account when setting your target.

You cannot predict injury.

You cannot influence somebody else's performance.

You cannot stop bad advice being given to you.

The fact that you cannot influence or predict someone else's performance is a good reason not to set an outcome goal. Your outcome is not solely dependent on yourself.

Aim for your TARGET.

Writing your target down is the first step to reaching it.

Using the criteria we have detailed and ensuring it is positive, what is your long-term goal?

Perhaps you could work on this with your coach or training partner.

Time

Assess

Realistic

Gain

Explicit

Task complexity

Double check your TARGET.

Is it a performance or process goal? Is it positive?

Now we have something to aim for, let's break this up into smaller challenges. Your short-term targets will be steps along the path to your long-term vision. If you set a target that is too far away, motivation may be lost. It is possible to lose sight of the end goal. This is why it is important to find smaller steps along the path.

You may decide on any number. These short-term goals can be both physical and mental.

Weekly Target:

A weekly target will show you that the ultimate goal is achievable and a daily target helps with day-to-day training motivation.

Choose four one week goals.

1 ....

2 ....

3 ....

4 ....

 Make sure the TARGET is covered.

These goals allow for periodic feedback and also allow you to re-adjust your overall long-term goal if necessary.

Daily Targets:

If you feel you need specific daily targets list them here.

1 ....

2 ....

3 ....

This book includes an entire chapter on Mental Imagery/ Visualisation. It is an important tool to the sportsperson and can also be used to increase your belief in your TARGET.

Any practice using mental rehearsal of what you will achieve is good practice, so when you have clear targets, visualise yourself hitting them.

What a lot of people don't realise is that goal setting is not a one-off event. If you continually revisit your goals, you are more likely to achieve them.

Conclusion:

Set your **GOAL** and accept it as your future reality. Commit to it. When you have read this chapter, set your goal and start moving towards your target. You will never again ask, 'Why make goals?'

Let's Get Going:

🔑 Time to Reflect and Put a Plan of Action in Place:

- What has been your biggest learning from this chapter?

- Select at least two tools which you are going to start using from this chapter and write them down in your log book.

1.

2.

- How and when are you going to start using them?

- How will this improve your performance?

CHAPTER FIVE:

NERVES

Paula Reinoso with Fernanda Sesto.

A triple Olympian (Atlanta 1996, Sydney 2000 and Athens 2004) who represented Argentina in fourteen World Championships and many other international regattas in the Women's 470 Class and Europe Class, both as a skipper and crew, over a successful sailing career spanning twelve years.

Paula's View of Nerves:

For me, adrenaline is great because at the end of the day it is what makes you keep doing the sport you chose. The mix of excitement and nervousness makes you super alert which is a good feeling and makes you want more. But too much nervousness can make you feel bad. The balance is important.

The techniques we used to manage the pressure were yoga and visualisation techniques. This was a very positive experience.

I remembered when I was seventeen, not being able to sleep because of nerves before a trial for the World Championship and being upset because I was going to be tired and would therefore underperform.

Later, I learnt not to fight the nerves, as it was worse if I did. Instead of worrying about being worried, (all negative thoughts) I tried to focus on the positive things like how hard I had being training and that I had done my homework. Therefore, whatever happens, happens. I also learnt that if I cannot sleep the night before a big day, there is no point worrying about it. I just start reading a book and wait until I feel sleepy again.

Paula's Sporting Success Tip:

Never blame something or someone else for the things that don't go right. It is a waste of energy and time. Move on quickly and try to focus on all the variables you can control.

The Secret Behind Nerves:

You have control over the thoughts you put into your head. You can control your nerves by adopting the right mindset and incorporating some mind training tools and techniques.

Science Behind the Secret of Nerves:

Decades of research backs up the theory that you are what you think. By this we mean, if you think you are capable of achieving more, you feel more positive and you become able to do more. If you tell yourself (think) you're a failure, you feel down and ensure you become a failure. When we relate this to nerves, if you tell yourself you always feel nervous and this becomes your focus, you are more likely to enhance this state. Whereas if you create a positive focus that you know helps you feel more confident and calm, you guessed it, you are more likely to be positive, calm and confident.

When we look at science, we can relate this to the placebo effect; that belief alone can heal the human body. Doctors know that by giving a dummy pill with no medicine in at all, it is possible to help patients with conditions ranging from angina and asthma to headaches and intestinal ulcers. When patients unknowingly take empty pill capsules, their belief that they will get better actually affects their physiologies. As we will continue to show throughout this book, the mind is powerful and science gives us evidence to illustrate this.

Unlocking Your Secret:

It is essential that adrenaline is present before you compete.

Having a sense of heightened energy, or if you choose to call this nerves, can help you perform.

It is essential to find the right balance of energy to enable you to reach your peak performance state.

You can control your ideal energy state by adopting the right mindset and incorporating some mind training tools and techniques.

"I used to almost be in denial before a competition which would then create a whirlwind of nerves before an event. I realised this was mainly because I didn't have a set psychological routine that would enable me to focus on myself and my preparation. This is now in place and it not only enables me to feel better before competitions, as my nerves are in control, but this also provides me with greater success." RG – British Champion Prone Rifle

"With nerves, we would focus on three things that we needed to do well and rehearse them time after time to make sure they felt right." Bryan Steele, four time Olympian

When working with clients, we start by looking at areas which may be holding them back. Nerves tend to be a part of the equation. The first thing we look at is the belief systems that surround 'nerves'. In this chapter we are going to examine beliefs, tools and controls to help you make a few tweaks which will enable you to unlock your true potential.

The first tool to introduce you to today is a very simple one. Let's throw the word 'nerves' out of your vocabulary. When you hear the word nerves, it can conjure up a feeling of fear and dread, and can be considered a negative word. However, if we realise that we need to have a certain level of energy to perform to our peak performance, it is essential that there is a level of anxiety. We need to control and embrace this.

Tool 1: Eliminate the word 'nerves' from your vocabulary. Let's call it something else. What is your new word? e.g. energy.

Tool 2: By changing this to a new word, does it make you feel differently when you think of that state?

When we look at energy, or your old and out of date word 'nerves', it is important to remember that we are all made up of energy and it is our choice how we use it. Energy is vital to our performances. Monitoring and controlling our energy is essential in creating our ideal performance states. So let's uncover what your ideal energy level is. Remember, everyone is different so it is important to identify exactly what yours is.

We start by looking back at your peak performance and understanding what your ideal energy level is:

My Best Performance:
Enter the location.

Before the competition:
Rate your energy level out of ten.

Ten being an exceptionally high energy state.

During the competition:
Rate your energy level out of ten.

My Worst Performance:
Enter the location.

Before the competition:
Rate your energy level out of ten.

During the competition:
Rate your energy level out of ten.

What were the main differences between these two performances?

Why was the energy level different?

What can you control and do differently now you know this will help you with future competitions?

What do you know now that you didn't know about energy before this exercise?

"The greater our fear of making a mistake, the greater the likelihood that we will make a mistake."

Sven-Goran Eriksson

Pressure:

Pressure and our perception of pressure can play a huge role in increasing our nerves.

Let's carry out an exercise to see if we can uncover any learnings which may help us in the future:

1. **Who creates your pressure?**

2. **Is there anyone you need to talk to; someone who can help you deal with this pressure differently?** For example, just before I race, my coach tells me the time I need to beat. This actually makes me feel really nervous and takes my focus away from my strategy, making me focus more on the outcome. I'm going to talk to my coach at my next training session and ask him to remind me of my strategy/process goals rather than my time before I compete. This will help me focus on the things I can control and the things which will enable me to be more present. With this, I will get the results in a way that makes me feel more confident and prepared rather than feeling pressured.

3. **What do I need to tell myself about the pressure I create and how can I deal with this differently now I know this?**

Dealing With Pressure:

Typical worries that can cause negative thoughts	Coping self-talk to help reduce negative thoughts
Demand worries The specifics of the challenge to be faced	
'This is a really intimidating ground to play at. The fans are really close to the pitch.'	'I've prepared really well this week, and this will be a great test to see how well I play with the fans so close to the pitch.'
'This team has been unbeaten so far this season.'	'All good runs come to an end. It would be great to be the team that beats them first.'
'This surface is really uneven and hard to play on.'	'Keep it simple, do the basics well and let the ball do the work on the surface.'
Ability worries Do we or I have the skills or experience to cope?	
'This is the biggest crowd I've played in front of. I hope I don't choke.'	'This is what I've been training for. I've created this opportunity. This is exciting and it's my time.'
'I just never seem to compete well in these conditions.'	'It is impossible to change the weather, so I'm going to take on this challenge.'
Consequence worries What you think might happen if things go wrong	
'If I have another average performance today, I know I will be dropped from the team.'	'Focus on the present, remember what my peak performance state is and what I can control. Relax and enjoy this opportunity.'
'I could really get badly injured on this surface today.'	'I'm here, I know what I need to focus on. It's time to get on with it and do my best.'

What are one or two changes/learnings you can pull from this and act upon today?

CHANGING HOW YOU THINK ABOUT NERVES	
UNHELPFUL	**HELPFUL**
1. 'I'm so nervous. I can't believe how I'm feeling.'	'This feeling of nerves and energy means I'm ready.'
2. 'I feel so sick and uncomfortable.'	'This is part of the build-up. Once I start, it will go.'
3. 'The time is going so slowly. This pressure feels like it is lasting for hours'.	'I'll take control of the time and use it effectively by doing visualisations to help me focus and relax.'
4. 'I've got so much nervous energy, I can't sit still.'	'This energy is building up, ready for me to compete. I'll channel this and use it to my advantage.'
5. 'I feel so tired with these nerves. I keep on yawning.'	'You know this always happens with important competitions. Just stick to the routine.'

What is an unhelpful thought you have heard yourself say?

What is a helpful thought you could replace this with?

How will this help you and when will you use this?

Changing Perfectionist Traits into Confidence Traits:

Another area we often see that affects a person's energy state is when perfectionist tendencies are adopted. It is important to realise that perfection does not exist in anything. Aiming for perfection can have a positive impact to an extent. It can help with drive, motivation and focus. However, there also comes a tipping point that can begin to affect confidence. If you are continually striving for something that does not exist without creating a sense of realism and balance, your confidence can be impacted.

Exercise 1: On the left column under the heading of perfectionist there are seven aspects listed. Just look at this column and circle any of these traits that you notice in yourself. Remember, this is the time to be truthful and realistic. As we said before, some of these have helped you in the past, but it might be time to start balancing these with those that may help your energy state.

Perfectionist	Confident Sports Person
High or strict expectations:	**Replace with manageable mini goals:** **My action/tool to help me with this learning is:** (for example - set mini process goals before each competition which will help me focus)
Dwell on shortcomings:	**Focus on strengths:** **My action/tool to help me with this learning is:** (for example - in my mind training book, write a list of all of my strengths to remind myself before I compete. This will give me confidence and help to focus my mind)

Fretting over past mistakes:	**Refocus on the present:** **My action/tool to help me with this learning is:** (for example - if I make a mistake, replay that shot in my mind, take a few deep breaths and focus on the present)
Self-critical behaviour:	**Own best friend:** **My action/tool to help me with this learning is:** (for example - create several positive self-talk phrases. Pull these from my peak performance chart or create some phrases that I know will help me)
Over analysis:	**Clear focused mind:** **My action/tool to help me with this learning is:** (for example - use my 3C Vision tool, covered later in this chapter, to help me when my mind starts getting busy and over analytical)
Easily frustrated:	**Lets go of mistakes:** **My action/tool to help me with this learning is:** (for example - adapt my evaluation questions and delete button to help me let go of mistakes. When a mistake happens, say the word 'delete', take a breath to get me present, replay in my head how I would do it differently the next time and then say the word 'focus' to bring me back to the present moment to move forward)
Focus on future performance:	**Focus in the present:** **My action/tool to help me with this learning is:** (for example - if my mind starts focusing on my future performances, I will re-evaluate my process goals and the things that I can control at that present time)

Taking Greater Control and Responsibility of Pressure:

What do I need to take greater control of	The things I can't control about pressure	My learnings/actions
e.g. Focus on my game plan or strategy.	e.g. Who I am competing against?	e.g. Instead of focusing on who I'm competing against, focus more on myself and my strategy so that I can work around areas that give me confidence, rather than things that create pressures that are not necessary or helpful for me.

My biggest learning about pressure has been:

Balancing Your Energy:

We have control over the thoughts we put into our head. To balance our energy, we need to be aware of stilling and controlling these thoughts. Remember, it's your choice and you are in control. Get ready to jump into the driving seat and take control of your energy levels.

Balancing your energy through your mental state:

Tool: What are one or two thoughts/phrases you could use to help you achieve your peak energy state?

Balancing your energy through your physical state:

Tool: Think back to your body language in your best performance. How were you acting before you competed? How were you holding yourself?

Remember, your mind can play tricks but you can also play tricks on your mind. It might be worth revising the confidence chapter and re-reading the body language section to remind yourself how you can take greater control of your body and how this affects your performance.

Where is Your Focus When it Comes to Your Energy?

So often we can focus on what we don't want to happen and as we know, our mind doesn't understand negatives, so by thinking, "I don't want to get nervous" you are loading your mind with the wrong type of message.

Let's take this learning and make it into a tool. It's important to realise that we can make a difference when we focus on what we want to happen. Ask yourself, "What is the most beneficial focus for you to have before a competition?"

Tool: My pre-competition focus:

My ideal focus for my strategy/plan before a competition is: Focus on my strengths and my game plan.

My ideal focus for my body language is:

My ideal focus for my self-talk is:

Is there anything else it would be useful for me to focus on?

Be Aware of How Your Language and Self-Talk Affects Your Energy:

The language we use can improve and also reduce performance outcomes in a number of ways. Below are some of the keys to this

- Be aware of your language and your self-talk.

- How positively do you talk to yourself?

- Do you help or hinder yourself through your language?

- Be aware, your subconscious is always listening.

- You have the choice of either setting yourself up for success or failure.

- Learn to be your own best coach by providing constructive and positive self-talk.

The Role of Our Subconscious Mind:

Let's remind ourselves how our subconscious mind plays a vital role with controlling our energy. As we've examined in the Thought Processes chapter, the subconscious mind houses an image of ourselves as an athlete. It is vital we put in the right thoughts, as our minds and bodies are completely connected. If we load our minds with negatives, this fuels our bodies with negative energy which can make it harder to perform. We can understand this mind and body connection more clearly when we examine adrenaline.

When your adrenaline is high, what things happen to you? Often athletes experience things such as increased heart rate, feeling sick, sweating, etc. The question you need to ask yourself is, "What thoughts are you putting into your mind that create this state?" There could be things such as "I need to beat my personal best" or perhaps you are focusing on other competitors instead of yourself.

In a single day, we have over one hundred thousand thoughts. How many of these thoughts are actually helpful and how many just create additional stress? Take time to distance yourself from the external chatter and calm your thoughts. A technique to help with this is imagining a 'delete' button. When a thought enters your mind that is of no significance, literally imagine pressing the delete button and replace it with a constructive thought like relax, or focus on what you are grateful for. The key is to start creating more time for your mind to be still and to increase positive thoughts.

So let's break it down so we can see how this works.

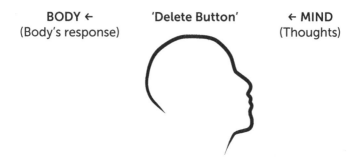

BODY ←   **'Delete Button'**   **← MIND**
(Body's response)   (Thoughts)

This diagram represents a simple way of looking at the mind and body connection. Imagine the head as a computer with positive and negative files, or perhaps an angel and a devil on your shoulder. Often, the positive thoughts gather cobwebs in the back of our minds instead of being at the front, helping to increase our confidence and focus.

Working with a recent client, an athlete who regularly became very nervous before a competition, we used this diagram to show how their thoughts were affecting their performance. When asked what some of their thoughts were prior to competing, they said that they would often think of all the things they did not want to happen in the race and the things that could go wrong. We then related this to the diagram. If I said to you now, "Don't think about pink elephants with yellow spots", what are you thinking about? Let me guess! The reason you are thinking about the elephants and the yellow spots, even though I said not to, is because your mind cannot hear negatives, therefore if you are loading your head with all the things you don't want to happen, guess what? You are telling it to focus on these things. You could fill your mind with negative thoughts and this can create certain beliefs; some may be fuelled by past significant events, or the language you use in your internal chatterbox. If you do this, the mind body connection will result in your body responding in a negative way.

So let's try a different approach. We worked with this same athlete to decide upon two thoughts that had in the past helped her perform well. With these two positive thoughts, her mind had a clear focus with clear instructions and her body responded in a confident and relaxed way.

Another option is to introduce a 'delete' button. If a negative thought begins to enter your mind, pause that thought and think of deleting it. For some people, they imagine that thought being blown up, the word erased or punched away. Get creative and find a tool that works for you. Remember, your mind can play tricks yet you can play tricks on your mind!

Now you are aware of your 'delete' button, you realise that you can start paying more attention to your thoughts, pause them and then delete them. You already have replacement thoughts or words you can draw from in your peak performance state. Notice that if you have a positive thought, your body also responds in a positive way. Try and feel really sad with a smile on your face and you'll see what I mean!

What thoughts/words or phrases can you put in your mind which will help control your ideal energy state?

Focus on Reducing Your Inner Dialogue Chatter:

As we've seen, controlling and reducing your inner dialogue chatter is really important, as your mind and body are connected and listening. How positive are you to yourself? Do you help or hinder yourself through your language? Be aware, your subconscious is always listening. You have the choice of either setting yourself up for success or failure. Learn to be your own best coach by providing constructive and positive self-talk.

Rate yourself out of ten on your self-talk: /10

To improve this score by two points, what would you need to change/improve?

What is the action you need to take to apply this change?

Is there a certain time when you might have to remind yourself of this?

How will this help improve your performance and make things easier for you?

Relaxation Techniques to Balance Energy:

Below are some techniques to play with. Find the ones that you feel will help you either before or during a competition. Remember to try and give each technique a chance. This chapter is all about finding a few techniques which will help you balance your energy.

Breathing Techniques:

If you focus on your breathing, you are unable to have other thoughts. This is a really simple and effective strategy to calm the mind.

Firstly, place your hand on your belly and a hand on your chest and breathe normally. Notice which area goes out as you exhale. Ideally you want to be breathing deep into your belly, as this will help circulate oxygen throughout your whole body and this deep breathing will enable you to be more grounded.

When someone becomes stressed, their breath automatically quickens, their breathing becomes shallower and they breathe more into their chest. By simply adopting some deep breathing techniques, you will naturally and automatically calm yourself.

Here are some additional breathing techniques for you to experiment with:

Technique 1:

- Inhale – Breathe in, fully focus on deep belly breathing.

- Hold your breath very briefly.

- Exhale slowly - and say the word in your head, "easy... easy...easy" with each exhalation.

- Repeat ten times.

Technique 2:

- Inhale – Breathe in fully and focus on deep belly breathing.

- As you inhale, for five breaths say the word "calm".

- As you exhale, think of letting go of any tension.

Technique 3: Alternate nostril breathing

- Inhale and hold one nostril closed by pressing on it with your thumb. As you exhale, use a finger from the same hand to hold the alternate nostril shut, as you exhale through the nostril which was closed with your thumb. Repeat this alternate nostril breathing.

Remember if you bring your awareness and focus to your breathing, you can stop your thoughts racing around. By simply adopting a breathing technique or building your own technique, you can achieve a greater sense of control, focus and calmness.

Props to Help Still Your Mind:

As we've seen throughout this book, keeping things simple, trusting your instinct and tuning into yourself are often the biggest keys to success. Below are some simple exercises to help you still your mind. It is important to remind ourselves and our minds to be more present and to live more in the moment, as being in the 'zone' is about being completely present. The more you control your mind and consciously are more present, you will become more calm and focused. This will also enable you to get into the 'zone' with more ease.

Here are two simple experiments to be done with another adult present in a secure area. Please also check where the fire alarms are!

- Light a candle, stare into it and let your eyes almost glaze over as you get lost in the flame.

- Sit in front of a fire and just notice the flames. Let your mind relax as you gaze into the fire.

- Sit still and focus on how your body is feeling. Really associate with it, perhaps your arm is itchy, maybe you can feel your back against the chair. Be completely mindful of how your body feels.

Get Back to Nature:

- Go for a walk in nature and just focus on your peaceful surroundings. Let in all the sounds and beauty of those surroundings.

- Locate a lake, river or the sea. Sit and just notice the peace of nature. Be aware how your mind just stills. When you leave, you will naturally feel calmer and more relaxed.

3C Vision Tool:

I was working with an international bestselling author of business psychology in the United States. I noticed before he went and gave one his talks to a sold-out audience, (and believe me, this audience was huge) he was staring at something on the wall for a few minutes. After the talk, I approached him and asked him if he had been using some kind of mind technique. He then told me about 3C vision. He explained that this very simple exercise enabled him to feel calm and focused, and he used it in all sorts of situations. Below is the technique he explained to me. Notice how it uses the breathing techniques along with the principles of being present outlined above.

- Take three deep breaths to still your mind and body.
- Choose your prop or find a point on the wall.
- Focus in on a small area on a wall or a prop.
- Notice how you can begin to see more out of the corners of your eyes (your peripheral vision).
- Let your eyes relax and they might begin to glaze over slightly.
- Let your focus relax on that point and gently breathe.
- Notice how calm, relaxed, present and focused you are.

Be aware that eventually after some practice, you can start incorporating props within your sport to help you achieve this state. If you are a tennis player, for example, you may be able to use the logo on a tennis ball; a football player, the stitching on the ball, etc.

Music/Audio/Video:

Music can be a very powerful tool to help aid relaxation and help create the energy state you want to achieve. We always advise that athletes create playlists rather than just listening to the radio or random songs, as then you can completely control the songs of your choice. Not just one playlist, but several for use in different circumstances and emotional states. For example, whilst travelling to the event, if your peak performance state is one of relaxation, create a playlist that makes you feel calm. Then before the event, if your peak performance energy state increases, set up a playlist that amplifies the energy to help get you in this state. Music can also be helpful when you want to relax and calm down before you switch off and sleep. A playlist for all eventualities!

Have you ever noticed that people tend not to disturb you if you have your headphones on? Whether you are listening to music or not, putting on your headphones is a useful tool if you would rather not be disturbed by others. Perhaps you could consider communicating this to your support team if you find it helpful when you are trying to focus.

Physical Relaxation:

We examine physical relaxation within our upcoming Mental Imagery chapter. Here is a summary of a technique to help relax your whole body. This technique may be useful to help calm your energy the night before an event or the morning of the event. Remember though, it is important to uncover your peak performance energy state to know exactly what level of calmness you need to create.

Work your way around every part of your body, starting with the top of your head, tensing every muscle and then relaxing it. Move down your face from your eyes, cheek bones, jaw, neck, working your way all the way down to your feet. Concentrate on tensing and relaxing each and every muscle. You could also anchor the word 'relax' as you let go.

Feelingisation:

Below is a summary of how you can use feelingisation to help balance your energy. Please also visit the Mental Imagery chapter to gain further insights into this area.

- Shut your eyes. Visualise and feel exactly what your ideal relaxation state is. You might imagine yourself on holiday on a beach with the sun against your skin, or in a place where you know you feel the most relaxed. Go through and really tap into what this feels like. As you notice the relaxation in your body, select a word like 'calm' and say this word to yourself several times, so this begins to anchor the relaxed state. Also, you can add a physical anchor, such as rolling your shoulders and letting them relax as you say 'calm'. Using both a physical and verbal anchor helps the mind and body connection increase the relaxed state.

Conclusion:

You have control over the thoughts you put into your head. To balance your energy you need to be aware of stilling and controlling these thoughts. Remember, it's your choice and you are in control.

⊶ Time to Reflect and Put a Plan of Action in Place:

- What has been your biggest learning from this chapter?

- Select at least two tools which you are going to start using from this chapter and write them down in your log book.

1.

2.

- How and when are you going to start using them?
- How will this improve your performance?

CHAPTER SIX:

MENTAL IMAGERY

Photo by Ady Kerry

Alex Danson – bronze medal Olympic medallist –
London 2012.

Alex's Use of Mental Imagery:

We produced individual 'winning formulas' that formed
our pre-match schedules for us to prepare and be ready
to compete. This consisted of elements from nutrition
and any specific actions such as packing my bag the night
before, to mentally preparing and visualising aspects of

my game. We then shared these winning formulas with everyone on our team, so we knew how to expect one another to behave and how others prepared for games.

I use sports psychology as a means of constant review and reflection. I keep a training diary in which I always document my pre-match targets as well as all my thoughts and reflections on these afterwards. This gives me an invaluable resource to look back on for instant feedback on games and also to see if any patterns of behaviours emerge.

I use mental imagery in a number of ways. I inject at short corners which is a closed skill, but one that requires perfect accuracy. I was very well aware that, although I could execute this skill in training, with sixteen thousand people at the Olympics, crowd noise would very quickly become a distraction. To counteract this, I had a very simple pre-performance routine that I used every single time I did the skill, whether I was in training or in a match. I then took this forward and used it throughout the Olympics. I closed my eyes for literally five seconds before I injected the ball and visualised the ball going in slow motion out to the exact spot I needed it to. In my mind, I felt the action perfectly and watched it accurately hit its target.

Another example of when I used mental imagery was after I suffered a subluxation to my right shoulder eight weeks before our first game at the Olympics. When you are injured, it is a very lonely place and negative thoughts can very easily take over your mind. Throughout those eight weeks I made myself spend time thinking about all the positive things I would be able to do at the Olympics. I thought about scoring and running back with my team mates. I visualised winning a medal and how it would feel to stand on the podium. This made me change my behaviour. Imagining myself in these situations helped me believe that I would recover in time. It kept me motivated throughout my rehab and meant I didn't lose focus at any point on what I so desperately wanted to achieve.

Alex's Sporting Success Tip:

We spend hours training our bodies to be in the best physical shape, but how long do we take to train our minds? Our body reacts as a result of what our mind is thinking. The biggest gain I made before London was controlling how I thought. This impacted directly on my self confidence and my ability to analyse my game and performance with a constructive eye. I used visualisation as a way to control my emotions and help keep nerves at bay. I think learning this skill had a hugely positive effect on my ability to execute skills and perform in a high pressured and highly charged event at the Olympic Games in London.

The Secret Behind Mental Imagery:

The brain cannot distinguish between an imagined experience and a real experience if you involve all your senses.

Science Behind the Secret:

Generally speaking, mental imagery is the process of creating a mental image or intention of what you want to happen or feel. It can be thought of as a controlled dreamlike state. Mental imagery can also be called visualisation, guided imagery, mental rehearsal, feelingisation and a number of other terms. The basic techniques and concepts are the same. As an athlete, you can use mental imagery to help you get the best out of yourself in competitive situations, training or performances.

One of the reasons that mental imagery can be so effective in performance contexts is that the brain cannot distinguish between an imagined experience and a real experience. A study that illustrates this was conducted in 1994 at Harvard Medical School which was known as *The Piano Study*. Volunteers repetitively played a five-fingered combination of notes on a piano. They did this for two hours a day for five consecutive days, while another group just imagined playing and hearing the same sequence of notes for the same duration of time.

At the end of the five days a brain scan was taken.

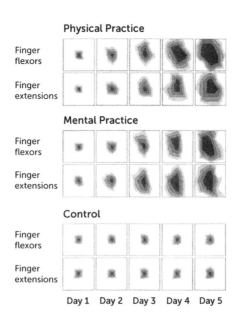

This brain scan shows that the finger maps for the volunteers who had played the notes (physical practice) had grown as expected, but remarkably, the maps for the volunteers who had just imagined playing them (mental practice) had also grown to the same extent.

This along with new scientific evidence shows how visualisation causes real chemical and physical changes in the brain and throughout the body. According to Dr David Hamilton, "The brain doesn't distinguish between real and imaginary. When you imagine something, the brain believes it is really happening. As we repetitively imagine our goal, this causes enough changes in the wiring of the brain, so that our thinking, what we say and how we act begin to change in the right ways to bring about what we are imagining."

Unlocking Your Secret:

⊶ Most athletes already use mental imagery naturally, though often not in a purposeful manner. When you repeatedly imagine yourself doing what you want to do, performing in a certain way and focusing on what you want to become, you are putting yourself on a path to create a more positive future reality. You are taking greater control of the process, which makes you feel more prepared. This in turn will make you feel more confident. When you back this up with the science that your mind doesn't know the difference between mental rehearsal and physical rehearsal, this is a huge key to creating greater success.

⊶ Similar to physical skills, mental skills need to be practised in a variety of settings, so that you can use them when they are most needed. In this chapter, we will provide you with various mental imagery tools for you to play with, to help you unlock your secret. Remember, as always to keep things simple, play with the tools and at the end identify which were the most effective for you and how you are going to incorporate these into your training.

⊶ The secret to success is taking control of your mind and thinking, to ensure that every possible advantage is being pursued. By using mental rehearsal, you help speed up the learning process and develop a new 'blueprint' of what you want to happen.

"Working with Katie has enabled me to realise that I have a personal library of video clips in my mind that I can use as often as I like. Part of my mind training routine is, before a competition, I imagine myself arriving at the tournament and running through my exact routine. I make the images as real as possible and particularly focus on how I would be feeling and thinking. I visualise my body language. I run through my warm-up routine and then go through the various matches. For me, this helps me feel so much more prepared and confident. Then when I turn up to the competition, I am a lot more relaxed and know exactly what my focus is, as in my head it feels like I have already been to the competition." LM – GB fencing

Having Fun with Mental Imagery:

- Imagine you are in a kitchen somewhere.

- On a bench is a basket of lemons. You reach out and select a ripe yellow lemon. You feel the weight of the lemon in your hand, you slide your fingers over the smooth waxy skin and feel the dimpled texture.

- You lift the lemon to your face and breathe in that lemony smell.

- Then you slice the lemon open.

- As the bright yellow flesh is exposed, you see the juice run out.

- A lovely lemony citrus aroma fills the room.

- You cut a slice and put it in your mouth.

- You bite down on it. The juice runs over your tongue and your mouth fills with the taste of lemon juice.

- Swallow the lemon.

Most people will find their mouth watering after reading the Eating a Lemon Visualisation exercise. This is because in order to make sense of what you hear or read, your brain has to retrieve the memories - the images, smells and textures - that the Lemon Visualisation brings to mind. The experience of eating a lemon is something that generates powerful physical reactions. Remembering eating the lemon recalls the distinctive reaction, and your body responds with a conditioned reflex. The Eating a Lemon Visualisation exercise demonstrates that words undoubtedly do have a physical effect on the body. It also demonstrates how powerful your mind is. Imagine how invaluable a tool it could be if you learnt how to use this to your advantage.

Arm as an Iron Bar:

- With a partner ideally of a similar height to yourself, face each other at arm's length apart.

- Have partner one rest an arm, palm facing up, on partner two's shoulder.

- Partner two link your hands around partner one's extended arm right above the elbow.

- Partner one is then instructed to tighten his arm so as not to let partner two bend it with her strength downward.

- Now have partner one imagine that starting from his shoulder his arm is a strong steel bar that extends through to the other wall.

- Give the partner at least thirty seconds to mentally imagine and feel the strength of their arm with this steel bar extending from their shoulder through to the other wall.

- When this image is created, have partner two push down on the arm like they did before.

In the vast majority of cases, when the image of the steel bar is created correctly, the arm is much stronger relative to the first scenario.

These fun experiments enable you to experience the power of mental imagery. Just by imagining that your arm was an iron bar, you gained some additional strength. Now just imagine what can happen if this same skill is applied to your sport!

"You get whatever you think about most."

Wayne W. Dyer

Mental imagery as a skill can be seen in many different sports. Some examples include:

- Watch how David Beckham pauses and focuses prior to striking a free kick as he prepares himself.

- Johnny Wilkinson during his conversion routine can be seen visualising the ball being struck through the posts before actually kicking.

- Nasser Hussain, when playing cricket, would go out in the middle of the pitch a day before a test match, as he visualised facing the opposition the next day and the tactics he was going to use.

- Tiger Woods, as he stands behind his ball, whether putting or driving, pauses to create an image in his mind of the shot he is about to play.

How Mental Imagery Can Help Unlock Your Secret to Success:

Mental imagery can be used to improve performance in a number of ways. Below are some of the key ways we've seen athletes achieve greater success by using mental imagery.

⊶ Seeing success:

You can create an image of yourself reaching your goal, how it would look and what it would feel like. This helps you build confidence, knowing that these goals can be achieved, and you can see yourself doing the things that take you to your end goal. This means that you then start to direct your mind to process goals, so it becomes a clear step-by-step route to reaching your final outcome goal (for more information, re-read the Goals chapter).

Increasing motivation:

If you need to increase your motivation at any stage during training, mental imagery is useful. You might create images of successful past events and future events, images of your goals for that session or beating a competitor to help increase your intensity level.

Managing energy levels:

Mental imagery can be used to alter energy states, using calming images to relax or energising images to psych up.

Reducing negative thoughts:

By focusing on positive outcomes, this will naturally increase positive thoughts.

Improving concentration:

As you have to block out irrelevant information when you are visualising, athletes often mention that because they are learning to control their thinking, they notice improved concentration in their performances.

Learning/perfecting skills:

Imagery can be used as an additional form of practice to help master a particular skill. It can also be used to correct errors in technique, either by reducing complex movements to simple skills or slowing the movements down to better analyse them for technique errors.

⚷ Refocusing:

During practice and competition, many distractions can arise that prevent an athlete from maintaining optimal focus. Imagining what to focus on can often help get an athlete back on track, by helping to remind them about what is important.

⚷ Preparing for competitions:

Just as an athlete needs to prepare physically for competition by stretching and warming up, he needs to get mentally ready. He can imagine himself in the physical competition environment and mentally rehearse key elements of his performance. He can also prepare for the unexpected by imagining himself in difficult situations and then seeing himself successfully dealing with them. Finally, he can also see himself succeeding. With a complete mental run-through of the key elements of your performance, you can set the stage for your desired pre-competition feelings and focus.

⚷ Familiarising:

As an athlete, you can use mental imagery to help you feel more familiar with a competition site, a race course, a complex play pattern or routine, etc.

⚷ Evaluating a performance:

After training or competing, imagery can be used to evaluate your performance. You can replay your performance in your head to reinforce what you did well and evaluate those aspects that need to be improved.

⚷ Recovery from an injury:

There are numerous mental skills you can use to help in the recovery process; imagery being one such skill.

Top Tips for Maximising Your Quality of Visualisation:

Be calm and relaxed: Imagery is most often effective when the mind is calm and the body is relaxed. If your body feels tense, take a few minutes to relax by focusing on your breathing and calming your body. If you get distracted while practising imagery, let the distracting thoughts and images float past as you reflect on the image.

Quick tip – If your mind is too busy for you to concentrate and focus, hold your tongue between your thumb and forefinger. This stills your tongue which makes very tiny movements when your mind is chattering away. This in turn will quieten your thoughts enough to allow you to focus on visualisation.

Use all the senses: Often, athletes only use their visual sense when they imagine seeing themselves perform. But equally important is feel, sound, thoughts, body position, and even smell and taste, as these are all part of the athletic experience. Paying attention to the detail of such sensations can help make imagery more vivid.

Control the mental images: In addition to vividness, being able to control images, making sure you see and feel yourself perform as you want to perform is another vital piece of successful imagery.

Keep imagery practice simple: It is generally best to first learn and practise imagery in a quiet environment with few distractions and play with the skill for about two minutes to start with.

"Whatever your mind can conceive and believe, it can achieve."

Napoleon Hill

Roll Up Your Sleeves and Let's Get Started:

We've broken the different uses of mental imagery into eight different sections. We'd suggest you run through all the exercises outlined below and then identify which two or three are the most helpful for you. Remember, keep things simple.

☞ One of the keys to your success is to remember that mental imagery has to be practised to be effective.

DIFFERENT USES OF MENTAL IMAGERY IN SPORT	THE AREAS I WOULD LIKE TO IMPROVE UPON
Practising specific skills in your head.	
Improving confidence and positive thinking.	
Rehearsing tactics or problem solving.	
Controlling pre-competition nerves.	
Competition preparation.	
Changing behaviours/habits.	
Competition analysis.	
Maintaining mental focus and positivity during injury.	

Let's Start to Create Your Mind Training Tools:

As we've mentioned, a key to the success of mental imagery is practice. When working with professional athletes, we scheduled ten to fifteen minutes of visualisation a day. We would suggest, for the most effective outcomes, a minimum of five minutes for at least four days a week. The great thing is, once you are familiar with visualisation, it is so easy to incorporate into your day, e.g. just before you fall asleep at night, en route to training (unless you are driving!), as you are getting changed, at training, before a competition, etc.

Simple introduction to the process:

- Sit in a comfortable place where you are free from disturbances.

- Relax your body and take four long, slow breaths.

- Close your eyes and create a vivid and convincing image of you playing your sport. This image can be one you've previously experienced or a goal you wish to achieve.

- If you become distracted or find you are thinking about something else, simply acknowledge the thought and let it go, then bring yourself back to the image.

- Focus on your breathing if you lose the image.

- Maintain a positive attitude.

- Feelings are key to mental imagery. We even refer to the process as feelingisation. Locking in how you want to feel is crucial in building your confidence.

- Imagine the sights, sounds, tastes, feelings and even the smells of the experience.

- Make the image and the scene as real as you can. Rather than looking down at yourself in the image, actually take part in the picture as you view the image from your own eyes to make it as real as possible.

- Take note of as much detail of the scene as possible. What are you wearing, who is there, what are you hearing, how do you feel?

- If your imagery session is not going the way you want it to, simply open your eyes and start from the beginning with your breathing.

- Accept sometimes it's just not going to work that day. It happens. Don't be annoyed by that. Tomorrow it will work. These days will become fewer with practice.

- Always end an imagery session with a positive image.

Remember, this is all about creating a plan that is right for you, so you might find that it is easier for you to visualise with your eyes open or standing up. As we've said, play with this and find what works best for you. You are likely to be already using visualisation to some degree, so build on this and tweak it with the tools and information we provide in this chapter to make it even more effective.

Different Uses Of Mental Imagery In Sport:

o— 1. Practising Specific Skills in the Mind

Exercise 1:

- Sit in a comfortable place where you are free from disturbances.

- Relax your body and take four long, slow breaths.

- Close your eyes and create a vivid image of you rehearsing a particular skill, e.g. creating your ideal shot/turn/putt/strike, etc., how it would feel, what it would look like and focusing on exactly what you would like to improve upon.

- If you become distracted or find you are thinking about something else, simply acknowledge the thought, let it go and bring yourself back to the image.

- Repeat this mental rehearsal for about two minutes as you see yourself in different environments, practising this skill. Make the images, sights and feelings really clear and fluid.

Exercise 2:

Often by imagining a specific subject, (object, animal, person) it can aid in your creation of images. Some examples of this are:

Runners - your legs feeling like springs as they feel light, springy and powerful.

Swimmers – feeling as if a current is pulling you forward as you feel yourself glide and propel through the water.

• Think back to when you performed at your best and the feelings this created. Are there any images which might assist you in a visualisation?

Skill:

Image:

How this image will help:

Shut your eyes and take a few deep breaths to calm and focus your mind and body.

Visualise your specific object or motion as it helps you connect with increasing your performance skill.

○━┳ Not only does the visualisation help with putting in place your new control programme, but you can imagine that the more you actually 'see' and feel yourself carrying out a skill successfully, the more likely you will be able to carry it out effectively in reality. This simple rehearsal of the skill in the mind lays down a picture of positive expectations, so that you have a positive perception of your ability to carry it out. Therefore, you feel more relaxed and confident about it. Contrast this with the athlete who constantly replays mistakes in his or her mind and repeatedly tenses up when in that situation, thus increasing the likelihood of that mistake recurring.

🔑 1. Improving Confidence and Positive Thinking

Exercise 1:

A good starting point to increase confidence through mental imagery is to identify your peak performance state.

We've looked at this in previous chapters, but we will run through this again to refresh your mind. If you have already completed this exercise, it will still be beneficial to run through it again.

An example of one your best performances:

- Where and when did this performance take place?

  Think back to this event and create a clear picture in your head of this performance as you remember what you were doing **before** you competed. This might be on arrival at the event, in the changing room, warming up or anytime before you stepped up to compete.

- What were you thinking before the competition? e.g. what were you focusing on?

- What were you feeling before the competition? e.g. adrenaline, prepared.

- How were you acting? e.g. body language, quiet/ chatty.

Now create a clear picture in your head of this event as you think back to what you were doing **during** the competition.

- What were you thinking during the competition? e.g. what were your thoughts?

- What were you feeling during the competition? e.g. excited.

- How were you acting? e.g. what did your body language look like?

An example of one of your worst performances:

- Where and when did this performance take place?

Think back to this event and create a clear picture in your head of this performance as you remember what you were doing **before** you competed. This might be on arrival at the event, in the changing room, warming up or anytime before you stepped up to compete.

- What were you thinking before the competition? e.g. what were you focusing on?

- What were you feeling before the competition? e.g. nervous.

- How were you acting? e.g. body language, quiet/ chatty.

Now create a picture in your head of this event as you think back to what you were doing during the competition.

- What were you thinking during the competition? e.g. what were your thoughts?

- What were you feeling during the competition? e.g. negative.

- How were you acting? e.g. body language.

- What are the main differences in the BEFORE column between both performances?

- What things can you control in your best performance state?

- What are your two keywords or phrases from your best performance state?

- What are some key thoughts, mental images and feelings that you could use to create your peak performance visualisation?

- What do you know now that you didn't know before you completed this exercise?

- Sit in a comfortable place where you are free from disturbances.

- Relax your body and take four long, slow breaths.

- Close your eyes and create a clear image of what you now know is your peak performance state. Before the competition, what are you thinking, feeling and acting?

- See yourself warming up before you compete and tap into your feelings of success that you identified in your peak performance state.

- Now see yourself during the competition, how you were performing and how you are taking control of your feelings. Connect to the feelings of confidence and what this looks like, how you are acting and what you are saying to yourself.

- Run through the competition in your head for about two to three minutes as you realise you can always create your peak performance state and enhance this by mentally rehearsing this state.

<u>Exercise 2:</u>

Before you start this exercise, think about a role model of yours and ask yourself, "Why is he/she my role model? What is it about their performance that impresses me?"

Now write down a description of their best performance:

- Shut your eyes and take a deep breath and hold it until it feels as though it's pulling at your chest slightly, then exhale. Now take a second breath which you take in deeply and let out normally to calm and focus your mind and body.

- Identify a role model/role models that you respect and who demonstrate confidence when they compete.

- Now visualise yourself performing in your sport with their characteristics and their confidence.

The aim of this visualisation exercise is that you see yourself responding and acting with the confidence and assurance of your role model. With practice, you will begin to associate yourself with these positive responses, rather than with the role model.

"I started this exercise by thinking of how they would handle the pressure. I'd match their body language and try to imagine how they thought. This has helped me identify with the attitudes that bring about success. I've found now that I naturally take on these behaviours." Jaguar Academy of Sport athlete.

Exercise 3:

Look at your trophies, video clips or anything that represents success at your sport to remind you of good past performances.

Make a list of some good performances to jog your memory.

After being able to easily recall at least five good past performances, then perform the exercise below. If it is tricky recalling good performances, it might indicate that you need to focus on these more, as it is likely you have concentrated on bad past performances instead. You need to switch some files around in your head and bring your focus to your good performances. Take the learnings from the not so good performances and then let go. Remember, wherever your mind goes, your body will follow. Make sure you direct your mind to what you want to happen, not what you don't want to happen!

- Shut your eyes and take a few deep breaths to calm and focus your mind and body.

- Replay highlights of your best performances in your mind. Think back to some of your performances, seeing yourself playing well and how you felt.

- These will serve as video clips in your head that you can keep adding to. You will then be able to play these video clips in your mind when you most need them.

⚷ 1. Rehearsing Tactics or Problem Solving

"A few days before a competition, I used to start visualising the upcoming event and rehearsing the various tactics I was going to use. I would just think about doing the perfect turn on the front and where we would put the power on or hold the power. We would go through this lots of times, making sure I could see my markers on the track when I did this.

As soon as I got to an event or track, I would try to have the perfect turn and know where my markers were. Then I wouldn't get nervous because I would focus purely on repeating this."

Bryan Steel – Olympic medalist, cycling

- Shut your eyes and take a few deep breaths to calm and focus your mind and body.

- Rehearse in your mind how to break down the tactics you are going to use in your next competition and see yourself performing these, or run through the routines you are going to use at your next training session.

⚷ Pre-competition Nerves:

- Shut your eyes and take a few deep breaths to calm and focus your mind and body.

- See yourself competing, playing well and positively and in your peak performance state – how you are feeling, acting and thinking.

- Use the five tools you identified that give you confidence (from the Confidence chapter) to include before you compete.

- Create positive images focusing on what you want to happen.

⚷ 1. Competition Preparation

Exercise 1:

- Shut your eyes and take a few deep breaths to calm and focus your mind and body.

- Visualise yourself performing at the location you are going to be competing at.

- Immerse yourself fully into the environment of the location; notice the sounds, smells, feelings, sights, colours, what you are wearing. What is going on around you? Really feel the environment.

- See yourself competing in different conditions, in different match situations and maintain your peak performance state of how you feel, act and think when you are confident.

- Now visualize the day going exactly as you want it. Go from start to finish in as much detail as you can imagine.

🔑 As we've seen from the fact behind the secret, when an athlete visualises the picture and the feel of a movement, there is electrical activity taking place in the muscles that are associated with the movement. Therefore the brain is actually mimicking firing the muscles in the patterns that are needed to execute the skill, but at a level that is not quite enough to make the actual body part move.

Exercise 2:

This can be used in the last thirty seconds just before you compete:

- Shut your eyes and take a few deep breaths to calm and focus your mind and body. (physical cue)

- Imagine a previous race win, see yourself winning and recreate those emotional feelings of success. (emotional cue)

- Return your focus to the start of the competition, thinking of blasting off the blocks/whistle/shot with the appropriate limb action. (focus cue)

"I've found the beauty of visualisation as a training tool is its portability. This form of mental training can be used during my off hours, during training, rehabilitation, or in the course of actual competition, particularly in those sports where there are intervals between event segments. I've found it to be highly effective in my sport."

SM - International F42 javelin athlete

⚠ 1. Changing Habits/Behaviours

Visualisation is also very helpful at changing behaviours which are not helping your performance. If for example you have a bad habit in your game that you want to change and you're having trouble physically changing this, by using effective visualisation, you can begin to alter a behaviour, setting up a new helpful habit.

- Write down an old toxic habit/behaviour which you would like to change.

- What are the benefits of this old habit? (Often there aren't any, but occasionally there might be.)

- Write down your new helpful habit/behaviour.

- Why build this habit/behaviour?

- What is the first thing you need to do to start this new habit?

- Shut your eyes and take a few deep breaths to calm and focus your mind and body.

- Now visualise yourself taking these first steps and seeing yourself using your new behaviour/habit and the benefits this is creating.

Notice how you are feeling and notice the improvements this has brought about in your performance.

⚬━ 1. Competition Review

The mental imagery techniques so far have focused on helping to influence performance in the future. However, visualisation can also be used after a competition is over. We have a recording of the competition in our heads and this is a useful exercise to scan through the images and review our learnings to carry into the next competition.

- Shut your eyes and take a few deep breaths to calm and focus your mind and body.

- Think back to the competition and replay the things that you did well in your head. Only focus on the positives, what they looked like and how they felt. If any negative images come into your head let them go and replace them with a positive image.

- Now visualise the things that you would do differently, if that competition situation were to happen again. See yourself performing differently, with the learnings you have taken from the competition.

Finish the visualisation pausing on an image of yourself doing something positive that made you feel confident in that competition.

O—r 1. Maintaining Mental Freshness During Injury

As we've seen, science proves that the mind doesn't distinguish between physically or mentally rehearsing something. This is a key factor when we examine injury and the role mental imagery has with the healing process and also with maintaining training.

Exercise 1:

- Shut your eyes and take a few deep breaths to calm and focus your mind and body.

- Visualise your peak performance state.

Exercise 2:

- Shut your eyes and take a few deep breaths to calm and focus your mind and body.

- Visualise ten of your best/good past performances.

Exercise 3:

- Shut your eyes and take a few deep breaths to calm and focus your mind and body.

- Picture yourself competing and training. Imagine the various skills and tactics to keep your mind focused and fresh during this time.

Exercise 4:

- Shut your eyes and take a few deep breaths to calm and focus your mind and body.

- If you have swelling, visualise a cold liquid around the area and see the swelling reduce. Adapt this to whatever injury you may have, e.g. bones healing, etc.

Find a quiet place, shut your eyes and take three deep breaths. Picture yourself in a performance situation using the two tools or learnings you have taken from this chapter. Notice how these tools are helping you improve your performance, how this feels and how this is bringing you greater success.

Conclusion:

It is really helpful when thinking about improving skills to bear in mind that a skill is actually controlled by the brain, and therefore the secret to changing and maintaining a skill is to ensure that the brain is 'reprogrammed' with new instructions. Once these new instructions are in place, it is much more likely that the body will readily reproduce the new pattern. Practice without reprogramming the brain will lead to an athlete sporadically showing they can execute the new skill pattern, but under pressure they will actually revert to their old habits. Mental imagery needs to be a central element of the process. Athletes recognise that they will also need to build up the time of their sessions little by little in order to get the best quality visualisation for as much of the session as possible. If you carry on sessions for too long, you can lose the quality of the visualisation and the session loses impact. Therefore, set yourself some time limits to begin with (e.g. two minutes) and focus on short, but frequent sessions rather than longer sessions carried out less frequently.

There is a vast amount of scientific research that shows, when it comes to helping an athlete develop a skill, the best way to bring this about is through a combination of actual physical practice combined with consistent visualisation. The physical practice ensures that the body and mind are getting used to working in harmony to produce the slightly different patterns of skill. This is then complemented by the visualisation sessions that ensure that the brain is beginning to restructure the subtle ways in which messages are sent to the muscles in order to produce the skill.

The simple rehearsal of the skill in the mind lays down a picture of positive expectations, so the player has a positive perception of their ability to carry it out, and therefore is relaxed and confident about it. Contrast this with the athlete who constantly replays mistakes in their mind, and repeatedly tenses up when in that situation, thus increasing the likelihood of that mistake occurring.

Remember, if you don't get on with mental imagery, then stick to using video clips of your performances. Recent research has shown that this can be just as effective as visualising, provided that you imagine being inside the image on the screen rather than just watching it as a removed viewer.

Simply identify the sequence/skill that is going to be visualised. Play the sequence on the DVD, pause it, and then visualise the same sequence, focusing on creating all of the sensory feedback that you would associate with what has just been watched. If you are using the role modeling approach, you would substitute yourself into that scene and feel yourself performing in exactly the same way that you had just seen your role model perform. In this book, we are providing you with a number of tools. It is all about finding the tools that work best for you. Everyone is different and so we have given you a number of alternatives.

As we've seen in this chapter, you have been given the opportunity to learn another psychological skill that will help you take control of your mind and your thinking, ensuring that every possible advantage is being pursued. As you build up your 'keys' to success in this book, you will be able to unlock your true potential.

⊙━ Time to Reflect and Put a Plan of Action in Place:

- What has been your biggest learning from this chapter?

- Select at least two tools which you are going to start using from this chapter and write them down in your log book.

1.

2.

- How and when are you going to start using them?

- How will this improve your performance?

CHAPTER SEVEN:

MOTIVATION

Nick Gillingham MBE, double Olympic medallist,
World Champion, World Record Holder.

Nick's View on Motivation:

To be motivated, you need to be confident in your ability,
irrespective of any concern over an outcome (end result).

I have learnt that motivation comes from passion, hunger
and desire. This is intrinsic of course, and therefore to be
motivated by others (extrinsic motivation) offers a difficult
quest (coaches, tutors, teachers, parents) which really is a

position of support. I learnt that a high level of support was often needed throughout each and every sporting season.

Self-belief is a strong psychological position which, to me, was and still remains, immeasurable. Looking back, I simply had an overwhelming sense of fulfilling my ability.

Motivated people should not fear failure, but see the target (goal) as an exciting and challenging opportunity. They have a 'want' (hunger) to be successful on a personal level. A sense of 'personal fulfilment' is highly important. In this respect, motivated individuals are fully committed to the processes and, as a generalisation, they are highly organised and analytical people who are often very critical of their performances (sport, education, business). These individuals work in the 'here and now' rather than the past or the future. I had a simple position and statement:

"I want to be better today than I was yesterday and better tomorrow than I am today."

Nick's Tip for Sporting Success:

Self-evaluation played a big part in my sporting success which has become a 'life skill'. I logged all my training sessions and outcomes each and every week across every training cycle for all the thirteen years I represented Great Britain. You need a plan. I found and need to constantly evaluate that plan and its processes. My log book not only recorded training sessions and all the associated sets and results, (outcomes) but information around 'life issues' in order to address balance. My log book also recorded all 'performance outcomes' in competition as well as the 'nuts & bolts' of racing, (reaction times, stroke rates, stroke count, splits, time differentials, break-out times and distances) in order to improve on my personal best next time, even if my personal best was already a 'world record'. I was constantly striving for perfection and wanting to set 'new standards' for the rest of the world to follow. I never settled for second best!

The Secret Behind Motivation:

Discover what drives you and you can increase your motivation.

Science Behind the Secret:

Research by Ryan and Deci (2000) recognised three different types of motivation:

Amotivation – a lack of motivation.

Intrinsic – where the motivation comes from an internal sense of fulfilment and personal autonomy.

Extrinsic – being motivated by external factors like accolades or to avoid the negative (carrot or stick).

Their research reflected, "Perhaps no single phenomenon reflects the positive potential of human nature as much as **intrinsic motivation**, the inherent tendency to seek out novelty and challenges, to extend and exercise one's capacities, to explore and to learn."

Research by Amiot et al, (2004) has identified benefits of being intrinsically motivated in sport.

In business and in many areas of life it has been shown that, for motivation to be sustained, the intrinsic goal is vital. Rewards and punishments have been seen as the most effective motivators in the past, but research by social scientists has proven this is not the case. For a person to reach their goal, there must be an internal desire to achieve or a desire to work for a team to achieve a goal.

Definition of motivation: 'Motivation is a psychological feature that arouses an organism to act towards a desired goal and elicits, controls, and sustains certain goal-directed behaviours.' Wikipedia

Some definitions of motivation make it sound like you either have it or you don't. This is not the case because motivation is like any other skill. It can be worked on and manipulated to achieve greater sporting performance. However, to do that we firstly need to understand the different types of motivation and which type is most influential for you as an individual.

To understand what motivates us and keeps that motivation in place, we will look at our **values**.

Values are the things that lie behind every element of what will drive you towards your goals. For example, if you value being a good friend, offering support to a friend in need will make you feel good. It's that value that drives you to act in a supportive way. If you value being a good parent, you will view your child's needs as a priority. If you value being a good sportsperson, you will ensure you act in a way that reflects that.

You may think that you are aware of what you value in life, but this exercise will open your eyes up to a broader range of values and also the level of value.

O━┳ Values Exercise:

Here is a list of life values. Take ten minutes to put these values into order of importance to you.

Rank them from 1 to 14 with 1 being the most important.

Love	
Security	
Success	
Health	
Excitement	
Fun	
Friendship	
Honesty	
Family	
Challenge	
Intelligence	
Control	
Courage	
Credibility	

When you did this exercise, were you surprised by some of your answers?

This exercise gives you a better understanding of what drives you. If you apply this same exercise to your sporting life, the knowledge you gain will give insight into what will motivate and sustain your inner drive.

Here is a list of values within your sporting life. Take a few minutes to list them in order of importance. Be honest with yourself. If you feel something is missing from this list, add it.

Agility	
Being the best	
Fitness	
Accomplishment	
Sportsmanship	
Mastery of your sport	
Love of the sport	
Financial gains	
Commitment	
Popularity	
The Training	
Support (coaches/team mates)	
Winning/medals/titles	
Adulation	
Self-satisfaction	

If a sportsperson has a high level of motivation, they will strive for their personal goals. If your motivation is low, then you will not train as hard. You will not push yourself to reach your goals and ultimately, you will underperform.

What is it that will drive you to go out training on a cold wet day?

What is it that will push you to work at 100% when you aren't enjoying it?

If two athletes or two teams have a similar ability, motivation may be the key to why one wins and the other loses.

We are concerned with two main types of motivation; extrinsic or external and intrinsic or internal.

Extrinsic Motivation:

Extrinsic motivation comes from external factors such as wanting to win medals, races or matches. This is driven by the desire for accolades, and rewards and recognition from others such as coaches, parents and team mates. How important were these to you in your list of sporting life values?

If an athlete is driven by extrinsic elements, he will also be motivated by the need to avoid punishment and disappointment. This can be highly motivating if used in the right way, but it can also cause problems, as those who are driven in this way can feel anxiety and nerves before performing and can be more affected by a poor performance.

Intrinsic Motivation:

Intrinsic motivation comes from your internal drive to complete a task and your personal enjoyment of the sport. People who are motivated this way possess self-determination.

Someone who has a high level of internal motivation will constantly challenge themselves, but this challenge comes from the love of the sport and every part of the sport. This type of motivation nurtures self-confidence and a feeling of satisfaction in the performance of the task in hand.

Both types of motivation are beneficial to a sportsperson, and you may have both driving you on. Usually, one will be stronger than the other and it is important to identify which is more prevalent for you. If you are aware of this, then you can tailor your goals in the right direction. For example, if you are driven extrinsically, it would be more beneficial to set a goal that heads towards an event, whereas those who recognise that their motivation is intrinsic would be better with a goal that is task-driven.

The other question to ask yourself is, are you aiming for something specific (approach) or away from something (avoidance)? If your coach tells you that if you miss one more training session you will be dropped, your motivation is external and you could use avoidance of this outcome to drive you on.

If missing training makes you feel bad about yourself and your relationship with your inner drive to succeed, then the motivation you find will be intrinsic and avoidance. The table below shows this more clearly.

Types of Motivation:

NEGATIVE	
MOVE AWAY FROM SOMETHING	
Intrinsic	Extrinsic
I really want to accomplish this for me.	Do all the work and you will have the title/medal
Intrinsic	Extrinsic
I really don't want to do this.	Do it or you are dropped.
POSITIVE	
TOWARDS A GOAL	

How important is it to you to excel in your sport at this moment?

0   1   2   3   4   5   6   7   8   9   10

Not important   Very important

Each sportsperson will need a combination of both internal and external motivations. At certain times, your priorities will change, and so it follows that the source of your motivation may also need to change. For example, if you have won a whole stream of accolades, then it stands to reason that external motivation will be influencing you.

So we have looked at the two types of motivation. We have found out what your personal set of values is and also your sports life values. This information leads to you knowing more about yourself and what drives you to succeed in your chosen sport.

Research by social scientists has told us that if a person has a high level of positive intrinsic motivation tied in with some emotion, they will find it easier to maintain their motivation for longer. To put it simply, if you have two players with equal ability, the one who has more intrinsic motivation will do better.

Let's unlock the secret of your motivation. Fill in the table below.

How would you feel if you didn't achieve your goal?	How would you feel if you did?

O—¬ Which are the most important to you from the list in the right-hand column?

Look at your goals and ask yourself, 'What is it that I want?'	'What could get in my way?'

O—¬ Look at what you have written down that you feel could get in your way and ask yourself, "How can I handle this so that it is no longer an obstacle?" For example – "I can't train for as long as I would like to due to other obligations." How can you overcome this?

Perhaps you could write out your average week and do a time-management exercise. It can be quite surprising how much time you can free up if you really want to.

Perhaps you could talk to your trainer about getting the optimum from the time you have available.

A few minutes brainstorming by yourself or with your trainer can often help you reframe an obstacle into something less negative.

O—¬ How to Increase Your Motivation:

1. Work through the values and sports values exercises in this chapter to discover what it is that drives you.

2. Completing the tables in this chapter will help you arrive at what it is that you actually want.

3. Make short-term goals regularly.

4. Manage you time to help alleviate outside pressures.

5. Look after your health and diet.

6. Put a training programme in place that includes plenty of variety; not just the type of training, but also differing lengths of time that you train for.

7. Include plenty of skills/process training, as these increase internal motivation.

8. Make sure some of your goals are skills-based. Once you have achieved a goal, your motivation will naturally increase.

9. Look at the people that are around you regularly and make sure that there are plenty of highly motivated people.

10. Accept that your motivation can have its good and bad days. When it's lower, then it will help to act 'as if' you were fully motivated.

Commitment:

When we look at and discuss motivation, it is necessary to also look at **commitment**.

Whereas motivation is intrinsically tied up with your feelings and emotions surrounding your sport, commitment means continuing with your task even if it's the last thing on earth that you want to do that day.

Where does your commitment come from?

Duty – It's what is expected of you.

Responsibility – To yourself or others.

Motivation – To goals, awards, the task, wanting it.

Accountability – Your efforts are recorded.

Habit/routine – 'It's what you do'.

Wouldn't it be great if we were fitted with gauges that could display our levels of internal motivation, external motivation and commitment at any given time?

🔑 How Can You Grow Your Commitment?

- Set goals regularly, daily, per session, weekly, to the next event, etc.

- Focus on what you love about your sport. Have pride in it.

- Learn how your mood and state of mind influences your focus.

- Concentrate on improving your skills.

- When you have stretched your limits, understand that the boundary has shifted and can shift again.

- Enjoy the sense of satisfaction you feel personally for a job well done, no matter how small.

- Recognise your dream and visualise it.

- Accept that you will constantly need to learn, but that journey can be very fulfilling.

- Increase your passion with every step.

- When you recognise a special moment, enjoy it.

The values exercise you did at the beginning of this chapter shows you what is important to you in all areas of your life. This information will only help a sportsperson if you then use it to determine your goals.

Motivation in Teams and for Coaches:

A coach has a specific role in team sports, and each will have their own style of leadership. If you imagine two teams who have similar strengths and weaknesses, it is the team with greater motivation and commitment that will be superior. Therefore, the coaches' role must include motivating the team as a whole, connecting and motivating the individuals within that team and increasing their level of commitment to the team.

Hollembeak and Amorose (2005) identified two major categories of coaching styles; democratic and autocratic. A democratic coach will listen to feedback from the players and will involve the team in their decision making. An autocratic coach makes all the decisions without reference to the players. Which approach do you prefer?

The impression a coach gives can have quite an impact on members of his team. Imagine a player before a big game. If he/she perceives a coach to be nervous, this will affect their own state and may also make them nervous.

Skill versus Ego:

There are two types of work environments created by the coach player relationship:

Skill-driven and ego-driven.

Skill-driven motivational environments concentrate on the

process of completing a certain task or skill and learning how to improve your skill level. The aim of this is to increase the effort on the task which will result in better performance. A coach who gives a lot of positive feedback leads players to view the environment as task-orientated.

Ego-driven motivational environments concentrate on winning as the main focus, with ability rather than effort as the answer to increased motivation. Players view the environment as ego-orientated if a coach gives less positive feedback.

🔑 It has been suggested that if a task driven environment resulted in players having higher levels of personal satisfaction, they were less likely to miss training sessions and also put more effort into those sessions.

🔑 All the research points to a democratic task-driven environment being the key for optimum motivation.

🔑 Remember that a team is made up of individuals. Some will be internally driven, some driven by external influences. Some will prefer task-orientated environments and others ego-driven.

Tips for Coaches to Increase a Team's Motivation:

1. Run through the values exercises at the start of the chapter to understand what values drive you.

2. Check your own 'motivation gauge'.

3. Even if your motivation is not at a high level, act 'as if' you were fully engaged.

4. Let your team see your enthusiasm and energy for

every aspect of what you are working on. If you arrive showing signs of boredom, how can you expect your team to be fully committed?

5. Develop a training programme that involves shorter sharper elements. Short bursts of fully involved team members will increase motivation more than long drawn out training sessions that allow a team member to lose concentration.

6. Give them and yourself some variety.

7. Reset goals regularly with individuals and the team as a whole.

8. Really get to know your players and what motivates them. Do they respond better to internal, skills based tasks or are they externally competitive with themselves and others? If you really know your team, you will know how to get 100% commitment.

9. Be consistent and fair.

10. Instilling a team spirit will help maintain motivation.

Conclusion:

A person's level of motivation can be affected by a number of internal and external factors, but these levels can be increased.

Once you have discovered exactly what it is that will drive you on to excel (internal) in your chosen sport, setting goals using this information will increase your commitment, helping you to be the best you can be.

🔑 Time to Reflect and Put a Plan of Action in Place:

- What has been your biggest learning from this chapter?

- Select at least two tools which you are going to start using from this chapter and write them down in your log book.

1.

2.

- How and when are you going to start using them?

- How will this improve your performance?

CHAPTER EIGHT:

COMMUNICATION

Rob Hobkinson – Performance Director with
Peak Golf Performance, working with elite golfers
including PGA tour players.

Rob's Use of Communication:

When you are working with people, communication is the foundation. It helps to pull the various people and personalities in a team together, building strong relationships, helping to ensure that the plans created are robust and appropriate, and also that the whole team is working towards the same thing in the right way. With open and honest communication throughout the team, you can make great progress towards your shared goal.

I find that people - and this includes athletes - can find it difficult to communicate the most important things, usually because they don't feel safe or comfortable enough to do so, or they think that this is 'personal' rather than 'work' related. People/athletes communicate the 'easy' stuff or alternatively keep feedback about plans/training approaches to themselves, thinking the trainer 'knows best'.

Therefore, besides working to create an open forum for communication - and that includes all team members - it is also important to realise it is not just what an athlete or team member is saying that you should be reading and paying attention to. Much of my focus on communication in my role is about observing and listening to the people I work with - picking up important non-verbal signals. It can often be what it NOT being said which provides insight into an important missing element. Taking note of how they are or how they perform in different situations and identifying these patterns can be really enlightening, helping to uncover missing elements that can make a real difference.

We learn from the way they behave in certain situations; their body language and patterns of behaviour.

For me, this runs alongside and supports the scientific aspect of my role and helps build a more rounded picture of something more meaningful in the long run, i.e. the overall well-being of the athlete. Elite sport can be a lonely and out-of-the-ordinary existence, meaning that successful athletes are often those surrounded by a supportive team. Part of my role is to ensure the team gels and continues to work through the varied peaks and troughs of performance. A key tool in achieving this is communication.

Communication is a highly important part of helping an athlete or team to achieve change, and in my view, ongoing change or development is necessary to move performance to another level.

Rob's Sporting Success Tip:

Great communication within a team can help athletes to cope with changes and get the rewards. Improving performance at any level is a journey and therefore the people around the athlete can be the guiding light to help them on their way. However, the athlete also has a responsibility to provide feedback, to communicate and to share their views.

To be successful in modern sport, you need to be physically, psychologically and socially happy. You are likely to be surrounded by a support network of people (scientists, managers, coaches, friends and family). Open communication between all these groups is important. Sharing of knowledge, experience and concerns are important. People often keep things close to their chest, seeing it as unrelated to their 'job' of performance. Not communicating these concerns to the rest of the team can be the detail that is crucial to the development of the athlete.

If you don't say it, people will make up in their heads what you are thinking.

The Secret Behind Communication:

Improved team and individual performances are directly linked to your verbal and non-verbal communication skills.

According to the Association for Applied Sports Psychology, 70% of human communication is non-verbal. www.Livestrong.com

---

Fact Behind the Secret:

Communication is a subject that is often overlooked, but with increased skills you can:

○━ Reduce the chance of misunderstanding.

○━ Gain greater influence.

○━ React positively to others.

○━ Achieve your goals, stating exactly what you want to achieve.

○━ Work well with others.

○━ Build solid relationships.

Communication skills can be learned and can give you greater control of any situation you find yourself in.

When we think of communication, we tend to refer to the way that we talk to people, but communication is so much more than that. First ask yourself:

"Who do I communicate with within my sport?"

Referees

Coach/trainer

Competitors

Supporters

Officials

Sponsors

Team mates

Physiotherapist

Sports Psychologist

Parents

Yourself

Do you use the same type of communication when dealing with each of these people? What is it that you alter?

There are a number of aspects of communication; verbal and non verbal, written, the way we respond, active listening.

Verbal Communication:

Communication comes in many forms, but when most people discuss this subject, they are referring to the way we speak to people, but even that involves a number of different aspects.

There are a number of variables that can affect the message you are conveying using speech:

- Pitch
- Tone
- Pauses
- Volume
- Pace
- Attitude/confidence
- Energy
- Rhythm and pacing
- Voice quality
- Emphasis on certain words
- Repeated phrases "You Know…" etc.

☛ Try reading the following sentence changing the emphasis to a different word each time you say it.

I did not say I couldn't

I **did** not say I couldn't

I did **not** say I couldn't

I did not **say** I couldn't

I did not say **I** couldn't

I did not say I **couldn't**

Have you ever had a conversation with someone who is totally disinterested in the content of what they are saying? If they aren't interested, chances are they will switch off and not pay attention to what you are saying. Whereas someone who has enthusiasm and puts energy and interest into what they are discussing is more likely to hold your attention.

O⊸ Here are a few tips to improve your verbal communication skills:

Lower the pitch of your voice to increase your authority.

Alter your pace depending on the message you are delivering. Speed up to add excitement and slow down to emphasise facts and create suspense.

Control your volume. Too loud, too often can irritate. Too soft and you won't be heard by everyone. If you have something important to say, try lowering your volume mid-speech or raise the volume unexpectedly. People will have to concentrate more. This shocks people into paying attention.

Choose your words carefully.

- Don't mumble, speak clearly.

- Repeat the part you want to make sure is remembered.

- Keep it simple.

- Know when to pause or use silence.

Non-verbal Communication

In the 1960s, Professor Albert Mehrabian conducted research into spoken communication and his results stated that when talking about feelings and attitudes:

- 7% of meaning is in the words that are spoken.

- 38% of meaning is in the way the words are said.

- 55% of meaning is in facial expression and body language.

- (source - NLP for Dummies)

This is an oversimplified understanding of his statistics because there are a few variables to consider, but the essence shows that facial expressions and body language are a very important part of communication.

A great example of the importance of body language is the Nixon vs. Kennedy debate in the 1960s. Part of the population listened to the debate on the radio and the rest watched it on TV. After the debate, people were asked who they felt had won it. The majority decision of those who had listened on the radio said Nixon had won, but those who watched on TV decided Kennedy was the winner. Nixon had greater verbal skills, but his body language made him appear untrustworthy. Whereas, Kennedy's body language was more confident.

The interesting thing about body language is that even if you are sitting in a room with others and not speaking, people will attach meaning to your body language. We are all constantly giving out signals that others will read in different ways. The majority of non-verbal communication is not consciously controlled, but you can become more skilled at reading it and using it to your advantage.

Body Language:

Body language and the understanding of how to read people is a wonderful tool to have, but you must always bear in mind that it is not an exact science.

Hands:

Your hands and their movement can be extremely expressive and can be consciously used to express your meaning or unconsciously to reveal thoughts and feelings.

- Palm up – indicates honesty and is a submissive sign. This evolved from centuries ago when you showed that you didn't have a weapon.

- Palms down – authority, strength.

- Hand on heart – you want them to know you really mean it.

- Finger pointing at someone – aggression, threat.

- Touching the nose when speaking – can indicate lying, exaggeration.

- Ear tugging – indecision.

- Hands in pockets – disinterest, boredom.

These are some classic examples of body language that show how you are feeling to those around you without even saying a word.

Can you read this boxer's body language?

Eyes:

The eyes offer us an opportunity to know a person a little better and to understand them without them even saying anything. If you ask someone a question, watch their eyes for clues. The eyes are wired to both sides of the brain and therefore move with the thinking process. Reading eye movements will allow you to discover whether a person is thinking using sounds, images or feelings. If you know this, then you can communicate with that person much more effectively. These indicators in the diagram below are true for the majority of people, but they are not an absolute and a small number of mainly left-handed people process this information in reverse, i.e. their eye movement will be a mirror image of what we have shown.

Eyes up and right can indicate that the person is constructing an image. They are seeing new things in their minds. A constructed image is not necessarily false and so is not an indicator of lying.

Eyes up and left can indicate that the person is recalling or remembering something.

Eyes right and down indicates a feeling. Eyes down and to the left indicates an internal conversation is going on.

If the eyes look centrally to the left it indicates a sound being remembered and to the right hearing new sounds.

Constructed Images — Remembered Images
Constructed Sounds — Remembered Sounds
Feelings — Internal Dialogue

Try this experiment

Remember a recent time you were with someone, training, competing or socialising. Ask that person to remember that time and watch their eye movement. Their eye movement will probably move up and to the left. If they do, then you know their eye movements will be the same as in the diagram.

Now ask more questions and note which way their eyes move, try to involve the other senses so that you can understand that person a little better.

Picture your favourite actor.

Imagine stepping onto snow in bare feet.

Think of the sound of church bells.

Having this additional knowledge gives you a tool that can be used to communicate using the same sensory language as the other person.

A visual person will use terms like, "I can **see** what you mean."

An auditory person may say, "That **sounds** OK."

The kinaesthetic person will ask, "Does that **feel** right?"

The person having the internal dialogue may not be focused on the communication with you. Being aware of that is an advantage.

When you become aware of your own system, the opportunity is then available for you to be flexible and adapt as you need to. Additional knowledge like this adds to your skills as a communicator.

How to Become an Expert Communicator:

John Grindler and Richard Bandler, the founders of Neuro Linguistic Programming – NLP, recognised that a person who is a good communicator has three main skills:

O— They know exactly what it is they want.

O— They pay attention to the response that they get, recognising that the meaning of the communication is the reply.

O— They have the ability to respond to this and change their behaviour to get their goal. Recognising that if something is not working, you need to do something differently.

They recognise that they are 100% responsible for the dialogue.

Games as You Have Never Seen Them Before:

When a psychologist refers to a game, they are describing a repeated cycle of behaviour with one or a number of players who take on and move between the Persecutor, Rescuer and Victim roles.

Have you ever heard yourself saying, "Why does this always happen to me?" or "Here we go again." This is a sure indicator that a game is going on.

When looking at the way we communicate, it is important to recognise if a game is going on and which role you are in. Games usually leave you feeling uncomfortable and de-motivated which is why we need to look at this.

The three roles in this cycle of behaviour known as the Drama Triangle are:

Persecutor   **Rescuer**

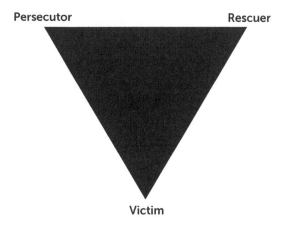

Victim

Here is an example of a fictitious scenario that demonstrates a game.

Helen: I really need to increase my stamina.

Coach: Let's put in an extra training session on Wednesdays to concentrate on your stamina.

Helen: I don't have time for an extra session.

Coach: OK let's add on fifteen minutes to a couple of the existing sessions and keep a log, so that we can track your improvement.

Helen: We could, but you know how bad I am at noting anything down.

Coach: I will set an app up on your phone, so that it will be simple and convenient.

Helen: I always have problems working phone apps.

Etc., etc.

In this example, Helen starts in the victim role and the coach offers all sorts of solutions from the rescuer position. When all of the coach's suggestions have been dismissed, the coach has moved into victim and Helen has become the persecutor.

People can switch roles and switch back again within one game. If you notice a game going on and it leaves you feeling put out and de-motivated, then the solution is to **step out of the game**.

In the example given, the coach can step out of the game by using a non-defensive response.

Coach: Yes you do.

If Helen is serious about wanting her stamina increased, she will have to come up with another suggestion, as the coach has left the game at this point.

This is an amazing tool for you and your skill as a communicator because games are repeated again and again, and now that you are aware of these games and the drama triangle, you will be ready with your response.

Ego states – Do You Respond Like an Adult, Child or Parent?

One of the skills needed to become a good communicator is to be aware of how you respond and how others respond to you.

Transactional Analysis was devised by Eric Berne in the 1950s as a way of looking at how we communicate with other people and also how we talk to ourselves.

He noticed that most communication responses could be put into three main categories

Parent Ego State – Behaviour, thoughts and feelings learnt from parental figures.

Adult Ego State – All actions, thoughts and feelings from the here and now. In this ego state, you look at the situation and make your decision based on the facts.

Child Ego State – Thoughts feelings and behaviours learnt in childhood.

When you respond from a parent ego state, your responses to others come from either the nurturing parent, "Have a day off training, you deserve it," or the critical parent, "Well, you didn't train very well today."

A response from a child ego state can be either from the rebellious child, "What do you mean I'm reserve? I'm not coming then!" or from the adaptive child ego state that just wants to keep the peace and do as they are asked, even if that's not what they really want to do. "I don't really want to go out Friday night, as it's an important game on Saturday, but they have made such an effort organising the night out, I don't want to upset them, so I will go."

The adult ego state looks at exactly what is going on, weighs up the consequences of a decision and then chooses what they want to do or say. When in this ego state, we do not make assumptions about people or situations. We see exactly what is going on. We ask for information and use what we have learnt from the past in communicating with others and ourselves, and make our decision being fully aware of the consequences.

Do you recognise any of these types of responses?

Let's see if you can recognise which egostate these statements come from.

Here's a quick reminder of the ego-states.

Nurturing parent NP, Critical/controlling parent CP, Adult A, Rebellious Child RC, Adaptive Child AC.

1) Well done. That was a great training session.

2) Why are you always late?

3) I will if you want me to.

4) So you think I can't do it, I'll show you.

5) I know this may not be a popular decision, but it's one I want to take and I know it's right for me.

6) That was a great performance. I deserve a day off.

Answers:

1) NP   2) CP   3)AC   4) RC   5) A   6) NP

Each one of these ego states can be a strength or a weakness. The rebellious child who uses this characteristic to move in a focused determined way towards their goal, the adaptive child who is happy just to follow instructions, the nurturing parent who continually tells themselves that they are doing well and looks after themselves, the critical parent that can drive you in the right direction, and finally the adult that looks logically at exactly what is going on and makes a decision based on the facts, recognising that it is their choice. These are all positive aspects of the various ego states.

What is really interesting is to watch and listen to others around you and see which ego state they are responding from. You can influence this and even move them into another ego state. For example, if someone is being critical, (CP) the expected and easiest response to make would be from the child ego state. If you continually respond from the adult, then eventually, they will also move into adult.

Try it out and see what happens.

Ego states is a huge subject and if you are interested in reading more about it we would suggest, *Games People Play* by Dr Eric Berne.

Communication Between Coach and Athlete:

"We are quick to paint a picture of a person on the first impressions. Yet people are very complex. It therefore takes an investment of time to fully gain a grasp of how our skills can be combined to achieve success. Therefore, having honest and open communication between the team is crucial. It is important the whole team is kept informed and take opportunities to feedback on what they are seeing when working with the athlete."

Rob Hobkinson – Performance Director with Peak Golf Performance

The Coaches' Perspective:

You could be the most brilliant coach in technical aspects and planning, but if you can't communicate your ideas and your perspectives, or you aren't able to motivate, you cannot succeed. Effective communication is the key to success as a coach/teacher. Therefore, we need to understand this subject and be aware of all aspects of verbal and non-verbal communication.

Keys to Effective Communication for Coaches:

O—π Pick the right time

When it comes to verbal communication, a key factor is recognising the right time to convey the message. The response to this message will depend on the recipient's ability to receive the message at that time. For example, immediately after a match with the whole team in attendance may not be the right time to talk to an individual.

O—π Be aware of the recipient

If you really know the person you are trying to communicate with, then you will also be aware of the right way to approach that person to get your message across.

O—π Set up your stall

What we mean is, an athlete or team needs to be aware of a coach's philosophy, attitude, expectations, guidelines and rules. If you want punctuality, then people need to know this. If you want an open door policy, then each individual needs to be confident that this is the case.

○━━ Be clear and consistent

If you have a policy of greeting each player in a positive way, then be consistent. Imagine what would be going through a player's mind if you always greeted everyone each day and then you totally ignored them one day. Consistency is crucial in the area of discipline if you want to be respected as a coach. This consistency also needs to include your body language.

○━━ Be empathic

Empathy means that you are aware of that person's emotional state and experiences, and can put yourself in their shoes, creating a full understanding of their position. If you are empathic with your players/athletes, then you will have a better understanding of the right way to communicate.

○━━ Look for signs that your message has been delivered.

> Remember, it is impossible to motivate
> without communication.

Team Communication:

"Communication, I think, is the biggest thing and you've got to have good communication with the players and with the coach and with the whole staff team." David Beckham, adapted from a transcript of an interview on Breakfast with Frost.

All teams are made up of a variety of individuals. To turn these individuals into a team that works together with commitment and cohesion, clear communication is essential.

Clear communication can change a mediocre team into an exceptional one. The more time a team spends ensuring that everyone has invested in their vision for the future, the more together that team will be. As previously mentioned in this chapter, a coach can use a different number of communication skills to discover the best way to deal with each individual member of a team. Some may prefer to have weekly one-to-one meetings, some may prefer to be directed rather than involved in decisions, others may only be really driven to perform well when they have been told they are not performing well enough, and others may perform better if they are encouraged. Some team members may learn team tactics using visual techniques, others auditory. How well do you know your players or team mates?

If you are a member of a team or are the coach, ask yourself:

Do you know exactly what is expected of you?

What are the team goals?

Have you contributed to all aspects of the team's focus?

Does your coach understand the way you like to be encouraged?

Have you built up a healthy relationship with your team mates?

Does the team feel like it is as one?

Are you a valued member of the team?

Are your opinions listened to?

Does your team have passion and commitment?

Let's break this down a little.

> Imagine that you were part of a dream team. Write down as many characteristics of that team and how it would feel to be a part of it as you can think of.
>
> e.g. team spirit   happy changing room
>
> mutual respect   support
>
> commitment from all   success
>
> non judgmental   equal playing field
> environment
>   social team

Take each one of these characteristics and place them in the table below. In the second column, rate which percentage out of hundred you feel your team has of that specific characteristic.

When you have decided which percentage your team has of each characteristic, look at them again and rate them 1-? with 1 being the one you feel is the most important to work on now.

Characteristic	%	1-?

Start with number one and see what differences you can make. If you do this exercise as a team, it opens up communication and clarifies all aspects of teamwork.

Conclusion:

Communication comes in a variety of ways, but it essential in all areas of your sport. The way we communicate and respond to others is a skill that can be improved by everyone of us, but to do that we must be aware. This chapter has covered why communication is so important for the individual sportsperson, team players and coaches. It has looked at who we communicate with and how we communicate. We have acknowledged that there are various ways to communicate, both verbal and non-verbal, and you have been given an insight into why we sometimes respond as we do.

⚿ Time to Reflect and Put a Plan of Action in Place:

- What has been your biggest learning from this chapter?

- Select at least two tools which you are going to start using from this chapter and write them down in your log book.

1.

2.

- How and when are you going to start using them?

- How will this improve your performance?

CHAPTER NINE:

EFFECTIVE EVALUATION

Ian Williams - four times World Match Racing Champion.
Ian has been nominated twice for the ISAF World Sailor of
the Year Award and twice for the British YJA Yachtsman
of the Year Award.

Ian's Use of Evaluation:

Performance evaluation is vital in any walk of life where
you are trying to make improvements. For me, the key is
to break performance down into the component parts in
order to effectively evaluate what areas need the most work
and where the easiest gains can be made. This is often to
copy another team that is performing better in that area.
If you are as good as the best team in each area, overall
you can be the best team without necessarily advancing
the state of the art.

When I was working my way up through the ranks, performance evaluation was also a big part of gaining confidence against the established teams. Once I realised we could match them in each area, then I knew we could beat them. As I have gained more experience, I have become better at understanding what is most important at that time. But that only comes with experience, so until you have that, you have to cover everything. I used to think, "How are we going to beat this team?" Once I knew we had all the necessary skills, the thought turned to, "How is this team going to beat us?" and once I could not see how they would beat us, they didn't.

Ian's Sporting Success Tip:

Sailing is such a complicated sport. There are many different approaches that can be successful. It may sound obvious, but it is important to keep focused on performance and how it can be improved, which is not always as easy to do as it sounds.

The Secret Behind Evaluation:

Effective written evaluation will speed up the rate at which your performance improves.

Science Behind the Secret:

The act of writing helps you clarify your thoughts, remember things better and reach your goals more easily. *Written Goal Study* by Gail Matthews of the Dominican University of California found that people who wrote down their goals, shared them with others and maintained accountability for their goals, were around 33% more likely to achieve them, versus those who simply formulated goals.

Writing stimulates a group of cells at the base of the brain called the **Reticular Activating System (RAS)**. The RAS acts as a filter for everything your brain needs to process, giving more importance to the things that you're actively focusing on at the moment — something that the physical act of writing brings to the forefront. In *Write It Down, Make It Happen*, author Henriette Anne Klauser says, "Writing triggers the RAS, which in turn sends a signal to the cerebral cortex: 'Wake up! Pay attention! Don't miss this detail!' Once you write down a goal or learning, your brain will be working overtime to see you get it, and will alert you to the signs and signals that were there all along."

Unlocking Your Secret:

○━ By creating a habit of effectively reviewing your performances, you will be able to take greater control of your confidence and your focus.

○━ The key is that you remove emotion from your evaluation and deal with the facts.

○━ Remember the importance of being positive and realistic.

○━ Turn your evaluations into learnings and then into actions.

Even though this chapter is at the end of this book, it might actually be one of the most important. We have broken up the book so you can work through the other eight areas and practise using the tools within them. This chapter shows you how to reflect and evaluate your use of these tools. Without doing this, you may sabotage the good work and changes you have created from the other chapters.

It is very easy to slip into the habit of coming away after training/competing and reflecting on the things you didn't do well, creating a negative feeling. If you do this, you potentially open yourself up to a lowering of your confidence and the creation of negative emotions such as frustration and anger. The key is to look at your learnings and then align these to your goals, or readjust your goals to incorporate these learnings. We are all capable of improving upon our performances, and with effective evaluation we can speed up this process.

"The road of life twists and turns and no two directions are ever the same. Yet our lessons come from the journey, not the destination."

Don Williams Jr.

We've created a very simple process which is quick, effective, and easy, and increases confidence and focus. There are some very simple questions to ask yourself after your performance which remove all emotion and enable you to get to the facts. You can add your own tailored questions if you wish to build on this.

The questions are simply:

1. What did I do well? e.g. I prepared well, stuck to my warm up routine, my first tee shot/touch/tackle, etc.

2. What would I do differently? e.g. speak to my coach as he said a few things that distracted my thoughts before I competed. We can then create a strategy together.

3. What gave me confidence? e.g. in my warm up routine I used the mind training tools to help me relax and this made me feel confident.

4. When was I most...? (You can tailor this to your specific goal e.g. focused, positive, relaxed etc.)

We encourage athletes to fill this out in the back of your log book. We would suggest you do this after every competition and after training. You might want to adapt this so you do it a few times a week after training or once a week after training. Find what works for you, create a plan and stick to it.

As we've said throughout this book, it is about playing with these tools and making them your own. You might want to get your coach or carer involved, for example, to help you with these questions, or you might prefer to do this yourself. Find the way that works for you and build on it.

We would also suggest at the end of each week you might want to add to your training evaluation questions. "Why am I better this week than last week?" Sometimes we might have to dig deep to find the answers, but this is when we know we are heading in the right direction and working effectively with our minds. We can always improve, yet it is important to give ourselves a chance to reflect and give ourselves a pat on the back along the way.

"There isn't a person anywhere who isn't capable of doing more than they think they can."

Henry Ford

Once you've pulled out your learnings, the next step is making them into actions. This might involve creating an action in your training the following week, e.g. what I would do differently – "At the competition I felt I was rushing and getting tense during my warm up. I want to have a more prepared and controlled warm up. I will discuss this with my coach in training on Monday and create a plan for this."

Conclusion:

By doing this evaluation and writing it down it enables you to feel more prepared, focused, professional and confident. Once again, do you see how we are taking greater control and responsibility of our performances and ourselves?

⚷ Time to Reflect and Put a Plan of Action in Place:

- What has been your biggest learning from this chapter?
- Select at least two tools which you are going to start using from this chapter and write them down in your log book.

1.

2.

- How and when are you going to start using them?
- How will this improve your performance?

CHAPTER TEN:

PRE-COMPETITION AND COMPETITION TOOLKIT

Sarah Winkless, Olympic bronze medal rower and double World Champion, Chair of the Athletes' Commission, British Olympic Association.

Sarah's View of Preparation and Mind Training:

For me, when I was preparing for a performance, there would be technical, tactical, physical and physiological elements.

As a small child, I was a 'girl' and had a brother who was fourteen months older than me. I quickly learnt that brute strength and even my natural speed was not enough to 'win'. I had many opportunities to observe how, with strategic thought, I could influence the outcome of a competition with him. I learned both by playing mental games of chess and tipping his mood by taking the 'horsey' (his favourite piece) and in other more physical games. I don't think I ever won a game of chess. I did learn that you could get your opposition to disengage or stop competing against you if you put them in a position that they didn't believe they could win.

Managing my own mind was a longer battle. Maybe being typically female, I struggled with my confidence. I was well versed in majoring on my weaknesses and working hard to eliminate them, sometimes losing sight of the strengths I had. Also highly competitive, I wanted to win at every opportunity, getting frustrated, downcast or even escalating to catastrophic thinking at what I saw as failures or my inability to achieve my own very high standards. Such instances could lead to my working harder and psychologically beating myself up. Due to the effort I put in, my performances improved. However, the journey was a bumpy one.

It was after I'd gone to my first Olympic Games in 2000 when I was lucky enough to start working with a sports psychologist, Brit Tajet Foxell, and we continued our work together until I retired in 2009. Through timely interventions, she taught me to work to 'train cleverer' rather than just looking to work harder.

I learned to control my mind just as I had learned to hone my technique and harness my power. The journey became smoother and my results more consistent. Training was still brutal and hugely physically demanding, and as with any athlete, I had my share of injuries and challenges to overcome. However, I was able to approach most situations using clear thinking which gave me a much greater chance of success.

Sarah's Sporting Success Tip:

Make sure you include mind training in your preparation, as clearer thought patterns give you a greater chance of success.

Secret About Your Toolkit:

Being prepared and creating your own personal mind training routine based around your exact needs will enable you to be more focused and confident, which will improve your performance.

Let's Create Your Toolkit:

Right at the beginning of this book, we asked you to get a small notebook/log book and to enter everything you would like to work on, including the two learnings at the end of each chapter.

This is how we finished each chapter:

O━ Time to Reflect and Put a Plan of Action in Place:

- What has been your biggest learning from this chapter?

- Select at least two tools which you are going to start using from this chapter and write them down in your log book.

1.

2.

- How and when are you going to start using them?
- How will this improve your performance?

Let's have a look at what you have put in your log book and collate the changes that you now recognise need to be made.

Chapter	Biggest Learning
Thought Processes	
Focus	
Confidence	
Goal Setting	
Nerves	
Mental Imagery	
Motivation	
Communication	
Evaluation	
Toolbox	

Now let's list those mind training tools that you identified from each of these chapters.

Chapters	Mind training tool 1	Mind training tool 2
Control Thought Processes tools		
Pinpoint Focus tools		
Build Confidence tools		
Setting Goals tools		
Reduce Nerves tools		
Master Mental Imagery tools		
Effective Motivation tools		
Improve Communication tools		
Facilitate Evaluation tools		

You may feel that some of these mind training tools will be best when you are training or maybe during pre-match/ competition. Some may be better during matches. This self-evaluation is important to get the most from this book and the tools and knowledge held within it.

Self-evaluation played a big part in my sporting success which has become a 'life skill'. I logged all my training sessions and outcomes each and every week across every training cycle for all the thirteen years I represented Great Britain.

You need a plan.

"I constantly evaluated the plan and its processes. My log book not only recorded training sessions and all the associated sets and results, (outcomes) but also information around 'life issues' in order to address balance. My log book also recorded all 'performance outcomes' in competition, as well as the 'nuts & bolts' of racing (reaction times, stroke rates, stroke count, splits, time differentials, break-out times and distances) in order to improve on my personal best next time, even if my personal best was already a 'world record'. I was constantly striving for perfection and wanting to set new standards for the rest of the world to follow. I never settled for second best!"

Nick Gillingham MBE, double Olympic medallist, World Champion, World Record Holder.

Mind Training Tools	Use in Training	Use Pre-match	Use during matches	Notes

Select your tools carefully and identify when they will be the most useful.

When we looked at Communication, we looked at who you needed to communicate with. Who needs to know that you are incorporating these mind training tools into your training and competition?

TOOLKIT COMMUNICATION	
Who do I need to communicate with about my plan?	
Is there anything they can do to help me with any of the tools/preparation?	
Are there any changes they could make?	

Now you have created your toolkit, we can create a simple routine for you. Simply fill in the details below:

Mind Training Routine:

Three Days/Week Before Competition:

e.g. meet with coach to finalise strategy, visualise my race plan for five to ten minutes a day, read through my best peak performance state.

-
-
-

Night Before Competition:

e.g. go through and check off my packing list, use my relaxation techniques, read through my mini goals for the day.

-
-
-

Day of Competition:

e.g. 3C vision, visualisation, focus tools.

-
-
-

After Competition:

e.g. evaluation, what I did well, what I would do differently, what gave me confidence, meet with coach and run through this and any of their suggestions, adjust goals as needed.

Conclusion:

We have looked at what your biggest learning is from each chapter, what mind training tools you are now going to use and when you will use them.

You have a choice of two paths ahead of you; one carries on as you are, while the other incorporates everything you have learnt in this book to improve your performance and be the best you can be.

"Some people want it to happen, some wish it would happen, others make it happen."

Michael Jordan

Katie Page BA (Hons), SAC Dip, SAC Cert:

I've had the pleasure of working with a wide range of athletes from Olympic, Paralympic, English team, professional, national, university, county and amateur level. My passion for mind and body connection began when I was diagnosed with an incurable virus which paralysed me when I was nineteen years old. Prior to this I had always been involved with competitive sports. I qualified for the GB trials for rowing and had been placed in the top three at the Junior Nationals for horse eventing. During the time I was paralysed I began researching the association between the mind and body. I was walking within nine months and my recovery baffled many doctors. I went on to qualify in sports psychology and multiple mind and body techniques from all over the world. I then moved out to America and developed corporate mind coaching programmes with Dr Spencer Johnson, international bestselling author, working with over half of the Fortune 500 companies. On returning to the UK I set up Mind Training For Sport and work with many of the top athletes in the UK. I have had the pleasure of working alongside many influential people in the sporting world which include:

- Dame Kelly Holmes DBE, MBE – Double gold Olympic Champion runner
- Katy Sexton MBE - World and Commonwealth Champion swimmer
- Zoe Baker - Four time World Record Holder and Commonwealth Champion swimmer
- Nick Gillingham MBE – Double gold Olympic Champion swimmer
- Sarah Winckless – Olympic bronze medallist rower
- Jamie Baulch - Olympic silver and gold at World Championships sprinter
- Dave Roberts – Eleven time Paralympic gold medallist
- Alex Danson – Olympic bronze medallist hockey player
- Tyrone Swaray - International sprinter
- Scott Moorhouse - International F42 javelin athlete
- Tom Davis – International judo player
- Alistair Heselton - Paralympic GB footballer
- Darren Cheesman - International hockey player
- Sarah Winckless – Olympic bronze medallist rower
- Alistair McKean - Paralympian bronze medallist rower
- Paula Reinoso - Sailing Olympian (Atlanta, Sydney and Athens)
- Mel Clewlow - Hockey Olympian (Sydney and Beijing)

- Hannah Beharry - International boxer
- Bryan Steel – Olympic bronze and silver medallist in track cycling (Sydney & Athens)
- Pippa Wilson – Olympic gold medallist in sailing
- Dave Alred MBE - Coach to Luke Donald and England Rugby Assistant Coach
- Peter McCraw – National Director of Coaching for Tennis in New Zealand
- Alison Rose – Physiotherapist to Jessica Ennis MBE – current European and former World Heptathlon Champion and World Indoor Pentathlon Champion
- Ken Blanchard – Regarded as the most influential leadership expert in the world
- Eddie Howe – Considered to be one of the best young football managers at this time
- Dr John Kotter – Professor at Harvard University regarded as an authority on leadership and change
- Dr Spencer Johnson – More than forty-eight million copies of his business books are in print worldwide. Advisor to the Centre of Public Leadership at Harvard's Kennedy School of Government

Helen Clarke Dip CH NLPP:

I left my role as an aviation broker, working in and around Lloyds of London to start a family and decided a change of career was called for. I have now taught English and Maths for the last eighteen years.

About ten years ago whilst still teaching, I retrained and began running counselling groups using Cognitive Behavioural Therapy and Transactional Annalysis. The difference you can make to a person's life and future continues to amaze me, even now after working with hundreds of clients during the last decade.

Having always loved sports, playing a variety at many different levels, I now work with a number of therapies including Clinical and Cognitive Hypnotherapy and Neuro Linguistic Programming. These therapies are effective in the treatment of a wide range of conditions from phobias to IBS, sleep problems, anxiety, pain management and any other area in which change is needed. I am a validated practitioner under the General Hypnotherapy Standards Council and am an Acknowledged Supervisor on the General Hypnotherapy Register.

In the sporting arena, NLP and hypnotherapy have been used for many years to help with sporting performance. They can greatly influence anxiety and confidence levels. Way back in the 1956 Australian Olympics held in

Melbourne, the Russian team took eleven hypnotherapists to gain mental clarity and help with visualisations.

I work with clients in this fascinating area to improve their sporting performance, help them reach peak performance state, focus consistently, increase confidence and self-belief, anchor these states and teach them to train their minds.